# FAIRYLORE

A COMPENDIUM OF THE FAE FOLK

# FAIRYLORE

DR. SARA CLETO & DR. BRITTANY WARMAN

STERLING ETHOS
New York

**STERLING ETHOS**
New York

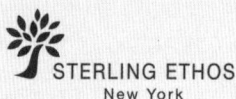

ISBN 978-1-4549-5880-2
ISBN 978-1-4549-5881-9 (e-book)

Library of Congress Control Number: 2025023388

Sterling Ethos books may be purchased in bulk for business, educational, or promotional use. For more information, please contact your local bookseller or the Hachette Book Group's Special Markets department at special.markets@hbgusa.com.

Printed in China

2 4 6 8 10 9 7 5 3 1

unionsquareandco.com

Cover and interior design by Stacy Wakefield Forte
Cover art and chapter opening paintings by Annie Stegg Gerard
Interior fairy drawings by Kristin Kwan
Interior images: Shutterstock.com: Vasya Kobelev (sidebar background art); Archive.org: Harold B. Lee Library (199), National Library of Scotland (219), University of California Libraries (135); Wikimedia Commons: Polish Digital Libraries Federation (10), Musées de la Ville de Strasbourg (97)

TO ALL OF OUR
CARTERHAUGH STUDENTS,
PAST, PRESENT, AND
FUTURE, AND ESPECIALLY
THE MEMBERS OF THE
CARTERHAUGH WRITERS
SOCIETY.

YOU BRING MORE MAGIC
INTO OUR LIVES THAN YOU
COULD POSSIBLY IMAGINE,
AND WE CAN NEVER THANK
YOU ENOUGH.

*contents*

**LEANNÁN SÍDHE**
IRELAND AND THE ISLE OF MAN

# FOREWORD

**B**ETWEEN THE SETTING OF THE SUN and the black of night, dusk is a potent, magical time, for in its eerie half-light—according to the folklore of Dartmoor, in England's West Country, where I make my home—one can cross the borders dividing the human world from the fairy realm. The twilight, or "dimpsy" as it's called here, contains powerful magic.

"Anytime that is 'betwixt and between' or transitional is the fairies' favorite time," says my Dartmoor neighbor, artist Brian Froud, an expert on local fairylore. "They inhabit transitional spaces like the bottom of the garden, existing in that boundary between cultivation and wilderness, or at the edges of water—the spot that is neither land nor lake, neither path nor pond. They relish moments of 'flux and flow': the hush between night and day, the times of change between one season and the next. They come when we are half-asleep. They come at moments when we least expect them; when our rational mind balances with the fluid irrational."

Dartmoor is a place where the old traditions of fairylore and belief have not died out. When I first moved here, an elderly neighbor learned of my interest in country lore and took me to visit "the fairy trees": a pair of otherwise-ordinary oaks standing on separate mounds of earth at the edge of a small wood. One of them had small strips of cloth ("clouties") hanging from the lower branches; this was the female tree, she said, and the clouties were a means of asking for wishes or blessing from the Hidden Folk. The other oak was the male tree; and that tree, she told me sternly, should never be approached, except by the Folk themselves. Many years have passed since that first visit and I have always heeded my neighbor's warning. Did my neighbor truly believe in fairies? Yes, she did—a belief that rested perfectly easily alongside her staunch Anglican faith. As for me, I believe in mystery; in the power of custom, ritual, and the stories that rest in the bones of the land; and in the way that passing on these things links us to the generations of the past and future. That in itself is magic.

You don't need to live in a place like Dartmoor, however, to encounter fairies, for the Hidden Folk and similar beings can be found all around the globe, taking many shapes and forms. Likewise, there are numerous ways to enter the "betwixt and between" of the Otherworld: Through fairy portals, gates, and doors in the hillside. Through the smoke of a bonfire on Midsummer's Night. Through the make-believe games of childhood, trembling at the edge of true enchantment. Through modern works of art, drama, and fiction inspired by old fairy traditions. But, as my elderly neighbor warned me all those years ago, fairies can be prickly, tricksy, and dangerous, and should always be approached with caution. It is best to seek out an expert guide to lead you into the realm and safely home again (which is not as easy as it might seem) . . . and I can think of no better guides than Brittany Warman and Sara Cleto. These two excellent folklorists have studied the subject in great depth, moving beyond the better-known tropes of fairy-lore to examine a wide range of

AN ILLUSTRATION
BY ARTHUR RACKHAM

fairy traditions the world over. They've explored the rich connections between magical beings, tales, and belief systems found in diverse lands among diverse peoples, while always honoring the cultural-specific aspects of each tradition. What I love best about Brittany and Sara's work (both in this book and in the folklore classes they offer through the Carterhaugh School) is their ability to take large, multilayered folklore subjects and present them in an accessible form. Their scholarship is rigorous, reliable, and satisfying to fellow folklorists, yet the warm, clear way they share their knowledge opens these subjects up to general readers, too, welcoming everyone in. They never lose sight of the wonder and enchantment that lies at the heart of these stories, and they remind us of why we need such tales today, perhaps more than ever.

In the Scottish fairy ballad "Thomas the Rhymer," the Faery Queen shows True Thomas three different roads that lie before them. One is narrow and edged with thorns and briars; that is the road of righteousness. One is broad and easy to travel; that is the road of wickedness. But there is a third road "winding through the fernie brae," a road that few will ever find. "That is the road to fair Elfland, where you and I shall go."

This book will set you on the third road: to Elfland, Fairyland, Tir-na-nog, and the other elusive lands that lie far beyond the fields we know. As you start your journey, here's advice from the tales of the country folk in Dartmoor: Put salt and rowan berries in your pocket. Wear an owl's feather in your cap. Wear your old coat inside out. Avoid the bluebells; they are enchanted. Don't eat the fairies' food. Be polite to everyone you encounter, no matter how humble or how grotesque. Don't make bargains; but if you must, follow that bargain to the letter. Keep your wits about you. Now turn the page, cross over the threshold. There is magic ahead.

—TERRI WINDLING

GWRAGEDD ANNWN

WALES, UK

# INTRODUCTION

# FAIRIES BETWEEN HEAVEN AND HELL

*Fairies being creatures of the imagination,*
*it is not possible to classify them*
*by fixed and immutable rules.*

—WIRT SIKES

The crisp autumn woods. The seashore, under the purples, blues, and golds of twilight. The ruins five miles outside of town. Caves deep and silent as a spell. The neon chaos of city streets.

Under your bed.

In your bed.

The underworld, under rocks, in the walls and streams and trees.

Look around. Look again.

Anywhere you've been. Anywhere you can dream up. That's where the fairies are.

# WHAT IS A FAIRY?

If you've picked up this book, we're willing to bet you have some kind of interest in the beings popularly known as fairies. Maybe you grew up loving fairy tales and dressing up in sparkling wings when you were little, maybe you're a huge fan of modern fairy stories like those of Holly Black or Melissa Marr, or perhaps you're a student dedicated to learning more about folklore around the world. Whatever the case, we want to challenge you with a question right off the bat: What even *is* a fairy?

It's a little harder to answer that question than you might think.

The word "fairy" or "faerie" has been around for a long time—since at least 1330 in English. In its earliest forms, "fairy" means something like "enchantment" or "magic," or a place that has those qualities. By 1375, "fairy" had expanded to include magical beings themselves—the kinds of creatures that you might find in those enchanted places. From the beginning, "fairy" has meant many different things: quality, place, creature. "Fairy" has always held the vastness of the human imagination.

But of course, "fairy" is not the only word that conveys these kinds of meanings. Around the world, fairies go by many different names. In Ireland, they're known as the Good People, while their Scottish counterparts are people of peace, the still folk, or even the silent moving folk. France has fées or

## MOOSELEUTE
GERMANY

corrigans. In Wales, you'll hear of the fair folk or the tylwyth teg, sometimes extended into y tylwyth teg yn y coed (the fair family of the wood) or tylwyth teg y mwn (the fair folk of the mine). Iceland has the huldufólk, or hidden people, and in Scandinavian countries you find trolls. There are many other generalized, sometimes overlapping words used for fairy creatures in English, too, including "fae," "gnome," "pixie," and "dwarf." These words are sometimes used with a lot of local specificity, but they can also function as catchall terms for big swaths of fairies. Another common word for these kinds of beings is the English word "elf," which may have derived, alongside the Old Norse word "álfr," from Proto-Germanic. In Germanic and Norse folklore, the álfr were spirits, and in the famous text the Prose Edda, these elves were even divided into two groups, light and dark. This very likely influenced the creation of the two different fairy courts in later Scottish folklore, the Seelie and Unseelie Courts. It's definitely not an easy task to untangle exactly how all of these words came to be as we understand them today, but suffice it to say that there are a *lot* of terms out there that seem to allude to very similar creatures and concepts.

Fun fact: Some scholars believe that J. R. R. Tolkien went with the word "elf" over the word "fairy" for the ethereal, long-lived, magical beings of his Middle Earth precisely for these complex etymological reasons, but that choice may also have had to do with wanting to get away from the typical Victorian depiction of fairies, which was still culturally dominant at the time he was writing. It's hard to grasp, now, how different Tolkien's fairies/elves were to an audience used to Victorian fairies, who tended to be small, cute, twee creatures.

It would also be a great mistake to assume that these kinds of beings are only found in the United Kingdom, Ireland, and the rest of Europe. In fact, there seems to be something very *human* in the desire to tell stories of magical folk whose influence can touch, and even reshape, your life. For instance, in Japan you'll find tales of the yōkai, supernatural beings profoundly entwined with the landscape and Japanese culture, and, at least in some ways, they mirror the fairies we think of in the US and Europe.

That said, as folklorists, we're going to be a bit of a buzzkill right off the bat and say that while universalizing is so very tempting, it's also usually pretty limiting and often erases crucial insights. A farmer in fifteenth-century Wales referring to a member of the "fair folk" is not equivalent to an American tourist visiting Ireland in 2022 and asking about fairies or a Japanese noble referring to yōkai in 1908. They all have different cultural baggage and different ideas attached to them. In other words, even the single word "fairy" has meant a lot of different things to different people.

To keep this book from spiraling out of control and being very confusing, however, we're going to be using the words "fairy" and "fairylore" throughout as deliberate umbrella terms. We'll use more specific language whenever we can, especially in the entries on specific magical creatures, but "fairy" is the most legible, recognizable word in the language in which we're writing, and we have to choose some word for cohesion. Basically, we gotta start somewhere, so we're going to go with "fairy."

## OKAY, FINE, BUT WHAT REALLY *ARE* FAIRIES?

Well, it's complicated. (Our students joke that this should be our tagline.) Andrew Lang, famous for his *Blue Fairy Book* (1889) and other anthologies of fairy tales, took a crack at this question by defining fairies specifically in relation to humanity. "Fairy," he says, is "the common term for a supposed race of supernatural beings who magically intermeddle in human affairs." In other words, in the stories Lang encountered, fairies are the supernatural creatures most likely to mess with humans, for good or ill. He goes on to say that "of all the minor creatures of mythology the fairies are the most beautiful, the most numerous, the most memorable in literature. Like all organic growths, whether of nature or of the fancy, they are not the immediate product of one country or of one time; they have a pedigree, and the question of their ancestry and affiliation is one of wide bearing." Lang is right that fairies and fairylike creatures are not limited to any specific time or place. They're everywhere, seducing humans or cleaning their shoes or terrorizing them in the woods under a new moon. And, as long as there have been folklorists and fairy enthusiasts, there has been speculation about what fairies really *are*.

It's been suggested, for example, that fairies are the product of a kind of shared humanity across times and places. This hinges on the idea that people globally share common stressors and challenges, and that fairies are an expression of those shared pressures (i.e., people everywhere are all the same, so we make and do the same stuff). Folklorists generally don't love this explanation, though, because it can be used to flatten and explain away cultural nuances or anything that feels unfamiliar to a Western audience. A similar but more sophisticated theory focuses on what we might call common structures. In other words, similar societies, with similar preoccupations and taboos, sometimes make similar stuff, including similar folklore. Finally, there's the idea that folklore travels (or spreads via what folklorists call direct transmission) and that's why you can find similar ideas around the world. For example, as scholar Diane Purkiss tells us, it was very possible for tales to spread across Greece and the Mediterranean and then into Germanic and Celtic regions, evolving and taking on local nuances along the way.

Across cultures, however, there are a few common ideas about fairies that seem to stick in addition to the conception of them as magical beings who commonly interact with humans. There's often a built-in assumption (especially in contemporary US culture) that fairies are always nature spirits or at least closely associated with nature. This, however, is absolutely not true across the board. There are all kinds of urban fairies out there, like the Japanese kamikiri, or hair cutter, who lurks pretty exclusively in city streets. Remember, fairies are, more than anything, a reflection of the people who

YUNWITSUNDI
CHEROKEE

tell stories about them, so any given fairy story is more likely to reveal how the *teller* feels about nature than any intrinsic connection between fairies and nature in general.

So where does the assumption that fairies = nature come from? Well, one theory is that fairies have been connected to elementals in various magical practices. Think, for example, about medieval magicians calling upon sylphs of the air, sprites of the earth, nymphs of the water, and salamanders of fire. It's easy to see how you could tie those kinds of spirits to fairies more generally. This also happens in contemporary pagan practices, like Wicca. Carole G. Silver adds that fairies can serve as explanations or even "personifications of disruptive forces of nature," but many of her examples are actually from literature about fairies as opposed to traditional materials. So while an association between fairies and nature can feel intuitive or obvious, and has been around for a long time, this connection only occurs "sometimes" and actually happens "more often in literature than in folklore," as Purkiss notes.

So, if the nature connection isn't 100 percent reliable, maybe fairies always look similar? Maybe small and sparkly, with wings? We're afraid to

**MUKI**
ANDES MOUNTAINS,
SOUTH AMERICA

break it to you, but, no, not even a little bit. There's no cheat sheet for this one. In the lore, fairies look like pretty much anything you can imagine. Truly, there are no limits. As folklorist Peter Narváez tells us, in traditional oral tales, fairies appear in everything from "red suits, [to] flowing gowns, [to] blue velvet knee britches, [to] long caps with peaks" and don't usually feature anything like "the diaphanous-winged, effeminate fairy images of literature and feature-length cartoons." Barbara Rieti calls fairies "protean beings" who can change "right before a person's eyes." Honestly, the most consistent thing about the way fairies look is that they reflect in some way the humans that imagine them, from aspects of their appearances, to how they behave, to the nature of their activities and obsessions, whether that's dancing, picking berries, conducting funerals, playing music, eating food, or wishing for babies. Ultimately, fairies are mirrors of some value, fear, or wish held by the people who tell their stories.

According to early fairy folklorist W. Y. Evans-Wentz, Welsh fairies tend to be small, pretty, and garbed in white, while in Brittany, France, "as a rule, [they] are described in legend as young and very beautiful. Some, however, appear to be centuries old, with teeth as long as a human hand, and with backs covered with seaweeds, and mussels, or other marine growths, as an indication of their great age." He adds that, according to an anonymous source from County Sligo in Ireland, "the folk are the grandest I have ever seen. They are far superior to us, and that is why they are called the *gentry*. They are not a working class, but a military-aristocratic class, tall and noble-appearing. They are a distinct race between our own and that of spirits, as they have told me [. . .] Their sight is so penetrating that I think they could see through the earth. They have a silvery voice, quick and sweet [. . .] They are able to appear in different forms." In the accounts Evans-Wentz collected throughout the Celtic countries of Europe, female, male, and fairies of no apparent sex are all featured, as are fairies that seem to be associated with different elements and different apparent moralities. His "wood beings," for instance, were often designated as good and helpful while "water beings" were evil.

An anonymous Irish mystic gave Evans-Wentz this vivid, distinctly elemental account: "The first of these I saw I remember very clearly, and the manner of its appearance; there was at first a dazzle of light, and then I saw that this came from the heart of a tall figure with a body apparently shaped out of half-transparent or opalescent air, and throughout the body ran a radiant, electrical fire, to which the heart seemed the centre. Around the head of this being and through its waving luminous hair, which was blown all about the body like living strands of gold, there appearing flaming wing-like auras. From the being itself light seemed to stream outwards in every direction; and the effect left on me after the vision was one of extraordinary lightness, joyousness, or ecstasy." So . . . there's that as well.

If fairies don't have any consistency in how they look or appear to humans, it's just as true with regard to their actions. In fact, the greatest consistency is inconsistency. Pro tip: If someone tells you "fairies are like X, always," they are extremely off base. It's perhaps most useful to think of fairies as *amoral* rather than as intrinsically good or evil. A fairy *might* help a human they encounter, but they're just as likely to ruin their night. They are not on the side of humans. They're really just doing their own thing that only occasionally intersects with humanity, usually for reasons of their own or happenstance.

One aspect of fairylore that comes up often is the danger of fairy food to humans, though even this can manifest in many ways. There's the idea that fairy food might not really be what it seems to be, or the warning that eating fairy food might trap you in their land forever. Sometimes, fairy food might be endless, manufactured via a magic tablecloth or similar; this food may or may not be wholesome, but you certainly won't be able to eat all of it! There's also a widespread tradition in which people proactively leave food out for the fairies, often in a bid to either win their favor or minimize the chances of their malicious interference.

ONI
JAPAN

While there are fairies who fear or detest humans, one pretty consistent throughline in fairylore is their *fascination* with humans. This is not necessarily a good thing for the humans in question! Fairies may show that interest through meddling, theft, or kidnapping, just as they might offer protection, new shoes, or a good time. There's also a persistent association between fairies and art. Fairies often love to dance or sing, but there's a big creative hiccup when it comes to making fresh material. While they might enjoy existing music or act as muses and provide inspiration, they (usually) cannot create anything new. They can only replicate what has already been done. For an example, we can look at Thomas Crofton Croker's 1825 version of "The Legend of Knockgrafton." Croker writes about a man with a hump on his back named Lusmore who hears fairy music. He adds a bit to their melody, and the fairies are so delighted and grateful to him that they magically remove his hump in appreciation. In this story, it seems that the fairies are so grateful to Lusmore because they have been singing the same tune over and over again. At first, Lusmore is so enchanted that he doesn't mind, but he soon feels "tired of hearing the same round sung over and over so often without any change." He then "[takes] up the tune, and raise[s] it with the words 'angus Da Cadine,' and then [goes] on singing with the voices." Lusmore, a mortal man, is the only one seemingly capable of adding to the tune, of making up *new* music for the fairies to sing. To the fairies, Lusmore's addition is an indication of how his "musical skill so far exceed[s] theirs," and they reward him. The implication seems to be that Irish fairy music is beautiful but limited by a lack of personal creativity on the part of its makers.

This lack of creative artistry is sometimes offered as an explanation for *why* fairies are so fascinated by humans: They covet human art, and so they kidnap human artists to get more of it. That may be why they go after great musicians so often, but really, any human is capable of making art, so, technically none of us is really safe from fairy kidnapping.

Fairies seem to have the most artistic power (even if it seems more like a magical power as opposed to a creative one) within the realm of dance. Through dance, they can entrap unwitting humans indefinitely and even kill them through exhaustion. We see strong strands of this in Eastern Europe and Russia especially, in fairies like the vila, the rusalka, and more.

# WHERE DO FAIRIES COME FROM?

Buckle up, friends, because fairies can be said to come from . . . well, a lot of different places. To make this as uncomplicated as we possibly can, we've divided everything up into what we see as the five major theories about the origins of fairies.

## IDEA #1: THEY'RE SUPER DEAD

Katharine Briggs tells us that, in the UK and Ireland, "the distinction between the fairies and the dead is vague and shifting" and that's . . . honestly a bit of an understatement. It's exceptionally difficult to tell whether certain characters of folkloric tradition, especially in this part of the world, belong to a separate fairy species or are meant to represent the spirits of mortals who have passed from this world to another. Folklorist Jenny Butler notes that "the connection between fairies and prehistoric burial mounds" adds another layer to all of this, too, supporting the argument that these ideas have been around for a really long time. So, are the fairies really just the dead? Folklorist Ray Cashman points out that "there has long been in Irish folklore a lingering conflation of the fairy Otherworld with the pre-Christian Celtic concept of Tír na nÓg (The Land of the Young), a timeless land where souls of the dead live in perpetual youth." Because of this conflation, fairies really can operate as one, the other, *and* both at the same time in these countries, and fairylike creatures from other countries around the world seem to often work in the same way. There is also the possibility that the dead live among fairies as well—as if sent to live with them as a kind of purgatory. Most of the time, specific kinds of dead people are said to experience this fate. Briggs notes "those killed before their time," "stillborn children," "long-dead or extinct races," and "the spirits of those drowned in Noah's Flood" all as possibilities recorded for that category.

Briggs adds that by the time W. Y. Evans-Wentz was collecting fairy stories in the early 1900s, "the greatest number of believers in all the [Celtic] countries spoke of them, though rather doubtfully, as the spirits of the dead." This seems to imply that there was at least a slight shift toward thinking of fairies as the spirits of the dead (as opposed to their own separate species) over time. We would argue that this fits with the modern inclination

to more readily believe in ghosts rather than fairies. Today, it's simply much easier to express belief in a ghost story as opposed to a fairy legend because culturally ghosts have remained somewhat plausible in a way that fairies, generally speaking, have not. There are many reasons for this that we can't really explore here, but anyone who's tried to tell others about a possible fairy encounter they had knows *exactly* what we're talking about!

**VELI**
FIJI

## IDEA #2: THEY'RE ANGELS WHO DIDN'T PICK A SIDE IN THE WAR

After Christianity became the dominant faith in Ireland, it became evident that there was a small problem: A large number of the locals still believed in the concept of fairies. The church establishment felt like they needed to come up with some kind of explanation for fairies that fit with a Christian worldview. In an attempt to blend the two ideas, as they often did, they declared that fairies were originally angels that had remained neutral in the war between God and Satan. When God prevailed over Satan, their indecisiveness meant that they were not bad enough for hell, but could not be allowed to stay in heaven either. As a compromise, God sent them down to live among humans on earth. There, they would retain some of their supernatural abilities, but would be punished by being forced to watch God's chosen people die with the potential to go to heaven, only to be barred forever from returning there themselves. Harsh.

As Ray Cashman points out, "The idea of the fairies as fallen or neutral angels—motifs F251.6 and V236.1 if you want to get folklorically technical—has a long history and wide European and even North American distribution," but it does seem to be an especially prominent idea in Ireland.

## IDEA #3: THEY'RE ACTUALLY SECRET DEMONS

Fairies have made occasional appearances in witchcraft trials over the years. Some church officials were clearly not comfortable with the semi-fallen angels idea and chose instead to cast fairies as essentially demons in disguise. Basically, as Briggs puts it, "all psychic experiences were deeply suspect" and "thought to be part of the diabolic machinery for ensnaring the souls of men." Fairies were sometimes recast as familiars—creatures that help witches with tasks like gathering eldritch materials, performing mischief, and casting spells. Witches and fairies could also be said to simply be in cahoots with each other—fairies would steal milk for witches, witches would steal babies for fairies, and so on and so forth. After the time of the witch trials, however, Briggs notes that it was much more common for Christian people in Ireland (and even parts of the UK) to believe in the "not good enough for heaven" and "too good for hell" idea, as we discussed above. We should also note here that some tales (like the Scottish ballad of "Tam Lin," which appears in our "Our Fairies, Ourselves" chapter) say that the fairies have to pay a tithe, sort of like a tax, to hell every seven years. Opinions differ on what that tax is for. It's possible that it was meant just to ensure hell leaves them alone, but it's also possible that Fairyland technically belongs to hell so they have to . . . pay rent? It's unclear, but the tithe itself is usually a mortal sacrifice, so definitely a little on the demonic side.

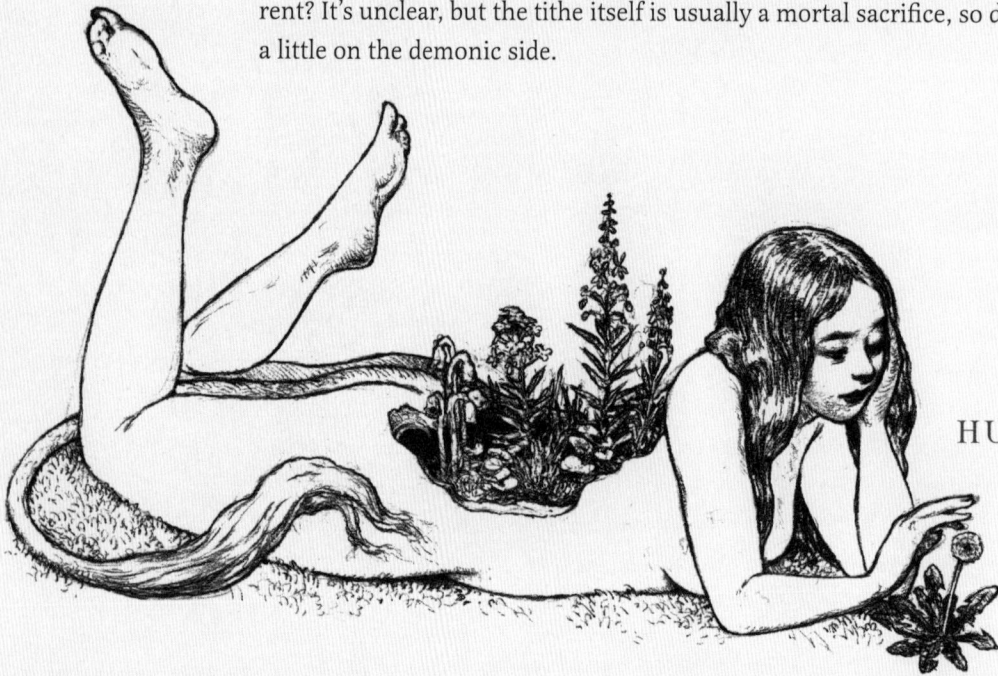

HULDUFOLK
ICELAND

Meanwhile, in the realm of fairy tales, witches and fairies often serve similar roles, such as godmothers providing essential items, villains ripe for conquering, and strange helper figures who may or may not have your best interests at heart. Preeminent fairy-tale scholar Jack Zipes discusses the "fusion and confusion of witches and fairies" in these tales and interestingly notes that while lots of fairy tales do feature fairies, "there are [ironically] hardly any fairies in the [famous] Brothers Grimm's collection"—instead, there are "witches, who [often essentially] function as fairies." He gives the example of the Grimms' "Rapunzel": He writes that the witch in this tale is "the mistress of the garden and forest who punishes a couple because they trespassed on her territory (sacred ground) without asking permission," all elements that actually link her to fairylore—a protective connection to nature, a concern about trespassing on sacred land, an emphasis on rules needing to be followed. This becomes even more tantalizing when one notes that in the 1812 first version of the Grimm text, the witch/sorceress of the 1857 version is actually called a "fairy"!

So why the switch? Well, there is probably a pretty concrete reason for this. In tales where there is a fairylike character, the Grimms avoided using that word, opting instead for words like "witch" or "wise woman" or "dwarf," depending on the situation. This is likely because the Grimms' fairy-tale collection was largely a nationalistic project. They were trying to prove, through folktales, that Germany had its own unique and rich background and history. As part of this, they were actively avoiding any perception of French influences, and fairies were perceived as coming from the French tradition as opposed to the German (even though that's obviously not true!). Therefore, if they found a story that mentioned a fairy, they just casually changed that word to something they perceived as more in line with German folklore. This conflation between fairies and witches in such an influential collection only heightened associations with fairies and the potentially demonic, essentially tarring fairies with the same brush used on witches.

It's worth noting, too, that in Iceland, the Huldufólk, or "hidden people," are also connected to this line of thinking. Briggs says that, in one popular story, God was visiting the earth and came upon a mother with a bunch of children: "The mother had only washed half the children, and she was ashamed of the others being seen dirty, so she sent them to hide among rocks and woods, and by streams. And God said: 'What you have hidden from me shall be hidden from Mankind.' And henceforth these children and their descendants became huldre-folk [*sic*], and lurked in caves or woods or streams." This seems to imply that here, too, fairies are if not demons or punished angels, then at least not blessed by God in the same way that mankind is. We'll talk more about Huldufólk in particular in the "Fairy Neighbors" chapter of this book.

## IDEA #4: THEY'RE NATURE SPIRITS AND/OR DIMINISHED OLD GODS

This idea seems to have gained popularity in the early 1800s with philologist Max Müller, who basically thought that all folklore (or at least mythology) started out as solar/celestial, which then diminished into the gods, and then diminished further into other folkloric creations like nature spirits, fairy-tale characters, and the like. Fairies were, of course, included in that assessment. Folklorists today don't put much stock in Müller's theory, but this one was definitely influential enough to be considered as part of what shaped ideas about where fairies came from. Evans-Wentz considered it "of very great importance" and, as Diane Purkiss notes, some thought it "possible to see in [fairies] reduced, tamed, Christianized forms of important deities" of earlier ages. Tempting though this theory is, it's simply not true (and certainly not in the broad, expansive way that Müller theorized). There are countless examples that don't fit, it's too simplified, and folklore, as we know, tends to be extremely complicated and resistant to such tidy answers.

That said, there's at least one area where the idea that some fairies may be the remnants of older gods does have some merit, and that's in Ireland. The Tuatha Dé Danann are part of traditional Irish mythology, and they're not *exactly* gods themselves, but they're god-adjacent. Their name even means "people of the goddess Danu," and while we know there was a goddess Danu in old Irish mythology, concrete knowledge about her is thin on the ground. The Tuatha Dé Danann were definitely a magical race, though, and they are sometimes said to be the ancestors of more recent conceptions of Irish fairies. As Jenny Butler notes, "The Tuatha Dé Danann became associated with underground fairies," but "a precise understanding of these mythical peoples of ancient Ireland is not possible due to the way these stories have been handed down to us." Basically, the material we do have was put together by "Christian scribes in the middle ages, so the beliefs and stories predate the assemblage of the material by hundreds if not thousands of years" and, even then, "it was partially recorded" and "mediated through a Christian worldview."

Finally, we should mention the nymphs, dryads, satyrs, and other creatures of Greek mythology here as well. In that worldview, as Purkiss writes, "nymphs [etc.] are caught between the world of gods and the world of men; they eat ambrosia, the food of the gods, but their lives, though long, are destined one day to end. Hence they are not goddesses [or gods], and like mortals they can suffer from familiarity with the gods." There are definitely connections to fairies here, right? Nymphs and nymphlike creatures are not gods, but they are magical; they're not immortal, but they live longer than humans; they're not worshiped exactly, but they're respected . . . all things that link them with common conceptions of fairies. There's also the fact that, often, nymph and nymphlike creatures are connected to specific natural elements, like dryads to trees. In fact, the strong association we have now between fairies and nature may have started with these creatures instead. Remember, Purkiss argues that the connection between fairies and nature is largely a literary construction, and Greek nymphs (etc.) might actually be where that association comes from. We speculate that Western European people, who were for a long time highly educated in Greek mythology, saw their own culture's similar creatures, noted those similarities, and proceeded to write things that explicitly made that connection.

TROLL
SCANDINAVIA

## IDEA #5: THEY'RE A LOST PREHISTORIC CULTURE

One last theory to go. As far back at least as the 1690s, the idea floated around that the fairies are possibly the remnants of a lost, prehistoric race of people, usually an earlier people of the British Isles. Evans-Wentz singles out the work of early folklorist David MacRitchie, calling it:

> the Pygmy Theory, which Mr. David MacRitchie, who is definitely committed to it, has so clearly set forth in his well-known work, entitled *The Testimony of Tradition*. This theory is that the whole fairy-belief has grown up out of a folk-memory of an actual Pygmy race. This race is supposed to have been a very early, prehistoric . . . race, which inhabited the British Islands and many parts of Continental Europe.

**KONGDERONG**
GAMBIA AND SENEGAL

This is supposed to explain things like why the fairies live away from modern areas and out in nature instead, why some fairies are smaller than humans, and even why some fairies were said to not be able to "bear cold iron: the ancient Britons were primitive and pre-Iron Age, and iron to them was the symbol of the people who had conquered them," as Purkiss puts it.

Okay, so, what do we do with this? Well, in some ways, this is a very appealing theory. As Purkiss notes, it allows fairies to be real, to "rescue them from story," as she says. However, there's pretty much no evidence that this is true in any way. In fact, a lot of what we think we know about ancient Britons is completely made up anyway.

That's the problem with our oldest preliterate societies. They just don't leave a lot behind to study. Many of the ideas we have about them come from speculations about the uses for stone circles and the imaginations of those with a vested interest in pushing certain ideas. Because of this, we tend to wind up with a "past-as-wished-for, in which a convenient selection of the evidence is fitted into a predetermined intellectual or emotional pattern," as archaeologist Stuart Piggot argues. Also, the few written sources we do have "are either external, in the form of Greek and Roman comments about aspects of Celtic culture which impressed them, or late vernacular texts, principally in Irish or Welsh, produced in a Christian environment," as folklorist Juliette Wood adds. So, basically, we just don't know enough to be able to say much of anything real about these ancient cultures.

There's also the significant problem that the idea of fairies being small is not universal in folklore or even especially prevalent. Fairies can be small, but they can just as easily be human sized or even bigger. The idea that fairies are tiny seems to have taken off in the days of Shakespeare and other writers of his period. As Purkiss says, "In their hands, fairies shrank to tininess. Though there are scattered references to tiny fairies in literature before Shakespeare, they are small rather than insect-like [. . .]. In the Queen Mab speech, Shakespeare gives the world fairies who come in shape no bigger than an agate-stone." Later, the Victorians would really run with this idea, but we'll talk more about that in our conclusion.

So, to sum up, absolutely none of these ideas is the be-all, end-all official origin for fairies, and, frankly, we're sure that there are a lot more possibilities out there, too. As folklorists, though, what matters most to us isn't where the fairies are said to have come from or finding the definite "right" answer, but rather why people are invested in this at all. Why does it matter so much where the idea of fairies came from? Why is *explaining* where they came from so often a part of their collective stories? We think it has a lot to do with justifying belief. If you can say where something comes from and why, doesn't that make it easier to believe in?

# WHERE AND HOW DO FAIRIES LIVE?

The questions of where fairies live, how their societies function, and how fairy time works all center around the idea of the liminal, or the transitional. Fairies are inherently creatures of liminal spaces, spaces that are neither here nor there, the betwixt and between. They live on the thresholds of the world. As Diane Purkiss writes, fairies are often associated with transitions: "birth, childhood, and its transitions, adolescence, sexual awakening, pregnancy and childbirth, old age, death. [They] presid[e] over the borders of our lives, the seams between one phase of life and another." This is reflected in where they live, how they live, and how they experience time.

## FAIRYLAND/FAERIE

Fairies may simply live among us, dwelling in the same forests and lakes and mountains that we know, but sometimes they live in a completely separate place that's for them alone. Fairyland, or Faerie—the separate realm exclusive to fairies—is a concept that crosses cultures. It may quite literally be a parallel dimension that exists alongside our own, one that you can pass into but not easily find on any map. It could just as easily be a place on earth that's difficult to find or get to—up in the clouds, out in the middle of the ocean, or underground. For example, we mentioned above that in Ireland, the world of the fairies was sometimes conflated with the concept of Tír na nÓg, the land of the forever youthful dead. That world, however, was not completely separate from ours like, say, heaven is in Christianity. Evans-Wentz puts it like this: "The heaven-world of the ancient Celts, unlike that of the Christians, was not situated in some distant, unknown region of planetary space, but here on our own earth. As it was necessarily a subjective world, poets could only describe it in terms more or less vague; and its exact geographical location, accordingly, differed widely in the minds of scribes from century to century. Sometimes, as is usual to-day in fairy-lore, it was a subterranean world entered through caverns, or hills, or mountains." He then adds that "more frequently, in the old Irish manuscripts, the Celtic Otherworld was located in the midst of the Western Ocean"! The Naga, a half-human, half-snake creature that appears in Hindu, Buddhist, and Jainist lore, "live in an underground kingdom called Naga-loka, or Patala-loka" which "is filled with resplendent palaces, beautifully ornament with precious gems." And in the Cook Islands, the beautiful Tapairu live in a magical pool that directly connects to Avaiki, the spirit world. Regardless of whether the land of the fairies is a part of our world or another, it is always a little different, a little strange: a place on the borders of our own. In other words, fairies congregate in places that are highly liminal.

## FAIRY SOCIETY

Within those worlds, fairy societies can take many shapes. W. B. Yeats divided the Irish fairies into two types—the "Trooping Fairies," who were the more social fairies, and the "Solitary Fairies," who do not play well with others. Yeats's trooping fairies had enough social structure to organize events like gatherings and parades. For example, Evans-Wentz collected a story from John Boylin in County Meath in Ireland, where he told him: "We were told as children, that, as soon as night fell, the fairies from Rath Ringlestown would form in a procession, across Tara road, pass round certain bushes which have not been disturbed for ages, and join the [. . .] host of industrious folk, the red fairies. We were afraid, and our nurses always brought us home before the advent of the fairy procession. One of the passes used by this procession happened to

**TAPAIRU**
COOK ISLANDS

## DULLAHAN
### IRELAND

be between two mud-wall houses; and it is said that a man went out of one of these houses at the wrong time, for when found he was dead: the fairies had *taken* him because he interfered with their procession." While this story might be narrating a trooping fairy gathering, it may also be about the Wild Hunt. Tales of the Wild Hunt and similar phenomena appear throughout Europe; they describe a supernatural group of hunters who go from place to place in pursuit of their quarry. These hunters can be fairies, ghosts, or a little of both. In many of these stories, humans unlucky enough to encounter the Hunt may get swept up and become a part of it. These humans may go into the Otherworld with the Hunt, as was apparently the case in Boylin's story, or simply remain permanently part of the Hunt, never able to leave. (People who die in mysterious circumstances were often said to have really been taken by the fairies to live in their world—the body left behind in these cases was commonly said to be a decoy of some kind.) Scholar Carole G. Silver notes that the Hunt betrays the fairies' "power as disruptive forces," their "bestial" and "wild" nature, and that it's possible to link conceptions of the Hunt to mob mentality. Technically (and unsurprisingly) the Hunt often functions as an omen, heralding the arrival of plague, war, death, or personal misfortune. We're guessing that the poor guy in the story above who happened to go outside at the wrong time would agree with that.

Sometimes we can see a much more structured concept of society for fairies, even extending to fairy kings and queens and their elaborate courts. This is perhaps most clearly exemplified in the Seelie and Unseelie Courts of Scottish folklore. Ceri Houlbrook notes that, in 1691, the minister Robert Kirk wrote about Scottish fairies that "appeared to be aristocratic in nature." They even, she adds, had "pastimes [that] reflected those of human courtiers." According to Skye Alexander, "Legends describe the Seelie [as] the 'blessed,' 'holy,' or 'light' fey"—basically, "good spirits who sometimes come to the aid of humans." On the other hand, the Unseelie Court was the home of "a bunch of bad guys bent on tormenting humans." Modern writers have really run with these ideas, and much of the contemporary fairy media out there draws on the idea of fairies having different courts, whether they be the comparatively simple "good" and "bad" courts of Scottish folklore or, as is often the case, seasonal courts where certain fairies are Summer Court fairies and others are Winter Court fairies. Today, we also see depictions that slightly alter the meaning of "Seelie" and "Unseelie" to center the amoral nature of fairies. In these depictions, the Seelie Court isn't necessarily morally good, but rather just the court that follows the rules to the letter, the court that honors the way things have always been done. As Briggs notes, traditionally, fairies "are great lovers of cleanliness, tidiness and established ways," after all. The Unseelie Court in these scenarios is more chaotic, more willing to break the rules and shake things up.

## TIME

Fairies often have what we might call an unconventional relationship with linear time. Time spent in Fairylands or even just with the fairies passes very differently than it normally does for humans. *How* differently is arbitrary and varies according to the story: "Sometimes a year is really nine hundred years, sometimes a night is twenty years, sometimes a few minutes' play [. . .] takes a hundred years or more," Briggs writes. She is careful to note, too, that "this timeless Fairyland is somehow interlocked with mortal time." For example, fairies seem to follow very specific rules that align with mortal calendars. Briggs offers temporal patterns like being rescued from fairies "after a year and a day," that "the fairies pay a seven-yearly teind to Hell," and that "a stolen changeling can win free in twice seven years" as examples. She also points out that fairies seem to be held to different rules at significant times of the mortal year, as "the times for seeing fairies or getting into Fairyland are [traditionally] May Day or Hallowmass," and that "certain times of day belong to them [as well]—twilight, midnight and full moon are times when fairies are to be seen." While most of our data here comes from Ireland and the UK, other fairylike creatures around the world seem to have similarly unconventional relation- ships with time. For example, in the Japanese fairy tale "Urashima Taro," the main character is spirited away to an underwater Fairyland where time also passes differently. When he returns home, over a hundred years have passed. So, once again, we find fairies in an in-between space: bound to mortal time but also separate from it.

## HOW IS A FAIRY DIFFERENT FROM A GHOST, SPIRIT, OR MERMAID?

Time for the million-dollar question: If fairies are so hard to pin down, if they don't all come from the same place, or mean the same things, or look the same way, or *anything* really, what makes them distinct from *any other kind* of supernatural creature?

Honestly, the division is incredibly arbitrary. What makes a fairy unique or separate from a goblin, a dragon, a vampire?

Let's try out a few greatest hits, the criteria we hear most often when we ask our students this question. Is it wings? Nope. Fairies don't always have wings. Classic Irish fairies don't have them, nor do brownies, nor many other creatures whose fairy status seems obvious. It's not being humanoid in shape. Think of standard fairies like will o' the wisps, which have no shape beyond glowing balls of light. It's not being little and Tinkerbell-sized. The Tuatha Dé Danann of Ireland? Human-sized or bigger. It's not being pretty or musical or connected to nature, either. About the only characteristic we see across the board is their connection to humans and their link to magic and the supernatural, which brings us back to square one.

This isn't to say that scholars haven't ever tried to narrow it down to more specific criteria. They definitely have. However, most of those efforts either rely on a focus on a particular region or resort to cherry-picking fairies to create a cohesive data set. Fairies simply do not conform to specifics on a more global scale. The truth of the matter is that there really is no neat or consistent rationale for separating fairies from other supernatural creatures. Because of this, we think the term is most useful as a catchall for magical creatures, similar to the way the words "fae" or "faerie" are occasionally used, too.

ALUX
MEXICO

For our purposes, fairies are folkloric, supernatural creatures who touch human lives, for better or worse, and that's what you'll find in the pages of this book. These are creatures that swim in the sea, ride with the dead, and dance through realms that might be Faerie or divine. They might shoot you, kiss you, or, if you're not careful, steal you away.

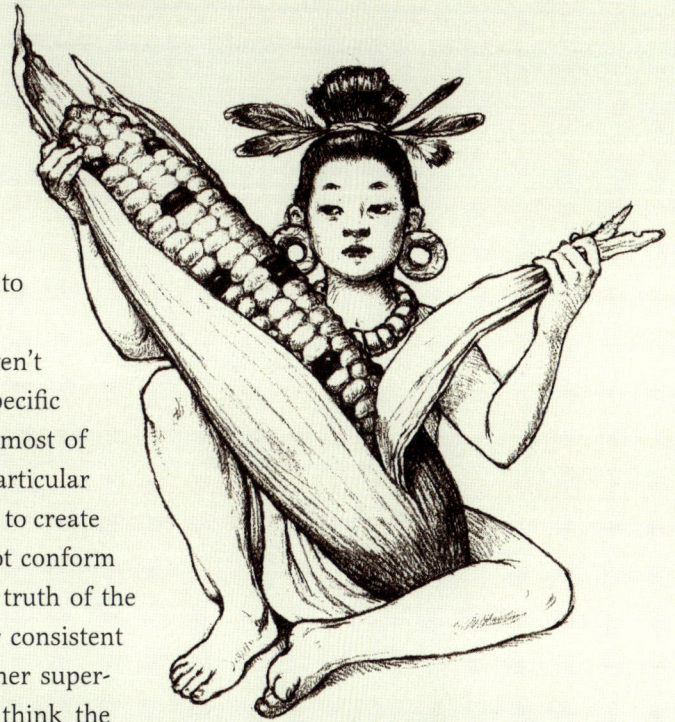

# A BRIEF NOTE ABOUT "FAIRY TALES"

Before going any further, we're going to put on our serious folklorist hats for a second. It's important to note that, from a folkloristic point of view, stories about fairies aren't usually "fairy tales." They're legends. Confusing? Yes, it is! We'll explain.

Stories from folklore about fairies—fairylore—are usually legends. Legends are set in the real world, in real locations, and they ask you to consider "Do I believe this or not?" when you hear them. They are stories with a "truth status" that is difficult to determine, so they shake up your worldview, your understanding of the world and how it works, a little bit! By contrast, no one thinks that fairy tales, like "Cinderella," are literally true and about the people who used to live down the street.

Fairy legends are like this: You hear someone talk about how they were out in the woods one day and saw a fairy who stole their scarf . . . then it's your job to determine whether you believe that story or not. Legends take place in the "real" world—our world—and often involve specific places that really exist, like England or Peachtree Road or the waterfall in the middle of Blackwood Forest. The fairies you'll find in this book, the fairies of fairylore, are legendary. They live in, or at least overlap with, our world; they interact in some way with humans; and they tell us things about our hopes, anxieties, fears, and wishes.

That said, we do also want to acknowledge that some stories about fairies can also be categorized as myths. Myths are stories that are considered to be deeply true on a sacred level. They're about big ideas like the beginning of the world or the creation of the first human, and they're often connected to spirituality and religion. These are the stories that are truer than true, and sometimes fairies make appearances. As we mentioned, the Irish Tuatha Dé Danann are a supernatural race that is, at least kinda, divine. In some stories, some of the Tuatha Dé Danann are gods

NUNO SA PUNSO
PHILIPPINES

or descendants of gods . . . which is getting into mythic territory. (Welcome to folklore! These categories are imperfect and will not always hold our fairies tidily!)

The last big, relevant folk narrative categories we need to mention are folktales and fairy tales. Fairy tales, which can be literary stories or a subcategory of the folktale, are stories that no one really believes to be true. They usually feature magic and take place "once upon a time" and "in a land far, far away" that is similar to but not quite ours. They can feature fairies as characters, but they usually don't. Why call them "*fairy* tales," then, you might ask? Well, the term folklorists tend to prefer is actually "wonder tales," but in the late 1700s, Marie-Catherine Le Jumel de Barneville, the Baroness d'Aulnoy, named her collection of these kinds of stories *Les Contes des fées* (*Fairy Tales*), and the name stuck hard. (Remember how we said the Grimms were trying to avoid the word "fairy" because of the French connections?) Even today, when we *know* it's not the most accurate term, we still use "fairy tales" because that's what's most culturally legible.

# SO WHY DO PEOPLE TELL STORIES ABOUT FAIRIES?

As we said, the stories people tell about fairies usually fall into the category of legends, but they can also veer into personal narrative (stories about their own experiences) and family narrative (stories about your family), too. Why? Because we tell fairy stories to make sense of things that befall us. They are a way of making sense of our world and our experiences.

Fairy stories can be a way to explain things with no ready explanation available. Why did Uncle Fergus die so young? Because he was such a good man and such a skilled fiddle player that the fairies stole him for themselves. Why did the baker lose his sight? Well, he saw something the fairies didn't want him to see. Fairies are especially likely to show up in moments of transition or danger, and they can be harbingers or explanations of disaster. They also can be a way to feel that you're exerting control in a chaotic world. If you treat the fairies kindly, if your local magical ecosystem is balanced, then peace may be maintained and disaster avoided. Fairy stories can be a way of dealing with tragedy or the unknown, too, especially death. This is why so many fairies blur with ghosts and the afterlife.

Peter Narváez puts this beautifully when he explains that fairies "demand appropriate responses rooted in traditional knowledge, for if ignored they may wreak havoc and disaster. Regional cultures, therefore, have evolved intricate rules of behavior on the basis of long experience with fairy habits, living spaces, likes, aversions, and ultimate designs." In other words, traditional fairy beliefs don't come from nowhere—they come from real dangers and concerns that societies navigate through attention to their landscapes. "Fairy liminality," he adds, "has prompted mortals to be cautious, observe prohibitions, and practice defensive and remedial magico-religious customs and rituals."

People have also told fairy stories as a way to explain deviant behavior or to avoid personal blame—basically, as a way to smooth and facilitate social interaction and to preserve community harmony. It's a way of keeping the peace by externalizing friction, and this can work in all kinds of different ways. For example, Narváez says that parts of the "changeling tradition stress the parental importance of such beliefs in assigning moral responsibility for the advent of disabled infants to fairy activities rather than to personal deficiencies. Thus, strong community beliefs in fairies have provided opportunities for changeling parents to coalesce with fairies by using fairy explanations in order to avoid the sanctions, embarrassment, and shame of other, more condemning traditional interpretations." Historically, it's been common for a visibly disabled baby to be understood as "cursed" by its parents' sins, especially the mother's. (Folklore can be pretty appalling sometimes, and changeling folklore is an especially rife area; more on this in a moment.) By saying "No, no, this isn't *my* child; it's clearly a fairy changeling," parents are attempting to exonerate themselves from one folkloric belief (the physical manifestation of "sin" in the body) by appealing to another (fairy interference). And this is only one example. Fairy stories can be, and have been, used as "alibis" for everything from chronic tardiness to premarital sex to infidelity to assault to even murder, and more besides.

Lastly, fairy legends caution as often as they explain—they're used to mark what's safe and what's not. And, as Narváez reminds us, most often, traditional fairy legends "functioned as agents of social control . . . Fairylore has maintained traditional values, therefore, by stressing the importance of subordinating individual desires to collective needs (obedient to community norms), and by underscoring the necessity of yielding to the wisdom of generational pressures (the admonitions of one's elders concerning fairies as threatening figures)." Much traditional fairylore teaches you how to survive physical and social danger, how to blend in, and how to conform.

This is, notably, pretty much the dead opposite of what most contemporary fairy enthusiasts (including us!) want. Nowadays, in the popular imagination, fairies are much more likely to represent rebellion, individuality, and being a social outsider. Why is this? How did this reversal come about? The answer is adaptation and pop culture. The fairies we see on screen, read about in novels, and see depicted in contemporary art now are fundamentally different from the fairies of folklore, which do usually serve as socially conservative forces. This, however, *feels* wrong to us because we're pretty invested now in fairies being the opposite of what they've most often been historically. Many of us are not embedded in these folkloric networks anymore, and the idea of fairies being forces of counterculture, rebellion, and social difference has been around for a long time. In fact, we have a theory that the tension between the "conservative" fairies of folklore and the rebellious fairies of our contemporary imaginations is frequently expressed through the idea of Seelie and Unseelie Courts in modern media (and that this is why the idea of those courts became so popular throughout contemporary fairy materials when for a long time it was just a pretty obscure idea from Scotland). The courts are a way to channel this

TENGU
JAPAN

disconnect between pop culture and folklore. The Seelie Court is a place of order and rule following, "good" but fundamentally conservative, while Unseelie Courts are socially deviant and rebellious. This split can hold the tension between the conservative fairies of folklore and the contemporary desire for fairies of change and rebellion, allowing them both to exist simultaneously in the popular conception of what fairies are.

## HOW WE'VE ORGANIZED THIS BOOK

Our goal is to make this book an academically informed and definitive reference to the world of fairies that is useful, bingeable, and beautiful. We want to capture the glamour and danger of fairies, not the sanitized versions more often on the shelf. The fairies of folklore are by turns frightening, sexy, amoral, silly, and powerful. Sure, sometimes a fairy will mend your shoes, but sometimes they'll come at you while carrying a whip made from a human spine. As we keep saying, they're complicated, and we want this reference to reflect that complexity and nuance.

Most fairy reference books available today contain one of two organizing principles: They either divide fairies by geographical location or present an alphabetical list. While both of these styles are useful, they do deemphasize the fascinating *connections* between the huge variety of fairylike creatures across cultures. For this reference, we've done something slightly different: a book structured around the different functions that fairies have (in other words,

**YAKSHA**

INDIA

what they do and what they mean to people), regardless of their location. Each chapter of this book is one way of seeing fairies, one way that fairies have been used to explain our world and ourselves. What fairies go in what chapter is, to some extent, arbitrary—almost all of them would fit in at least one other chapter because fairies are never just one thing! They'd be (im)mortally offended at the very notion. But our goal was to foreground what fairies mean to people and the patterns that emerge again and again in fairy legends.

For example, there are numerous fairies around the world whose main function is the seduction of humans. The Irish leannán sídhe (who sucks the life force from young artists and poets in exchange for providing muse-like inspiration), the Filipino tamawo (who steal human women to live with them in their parallel fairy world), and the nikusui of Japan (the femme-fatale yōkai who suck the flesh from their victims' bones and, incidentally, share their name with a popular soup) can all be grouped together in this way.

We believe that this approach highlights why these fairies matter so much culturally. It allows us to go more in depth into each individual fairy and emphasizes the things that connect them to humanity, to *us*. As we've said, ultimately the most interesting thing about fairies is that they are a way for people to speak about the world, their own experiences, and their own lives. To that point, we've also included a short story from folklore or inspired by folklore in each chapter.

A few caveats before we begin. First, we know that this approach means that we cannot include every fairy from every source. To echo what scholar Diane Purkiss perfectly notes in her acknowledgments for her book *At the Bottom of the Garden*, "This book is an imperfect . . . creature," and while "some fairies will be very offended at not finding their names here," we simply cannot include them all, and because we "do not pretend to include all, [. . .] no exclusions should seem hurtful." We also do not speak every language in the world (though how we wish we did!), and have mostly relied on English sources for this text. For a variety of reasons—the most important one being the historical fact that colonialism often results in the obfuscation of traditional culture or tries to make it fit with the pre-existing notions of the dominant culture (including the Western idea of what a fairy even is)—we recognize that we may not have everything 100 percent right. We have endeavored to consult the best sources we could find (and note when the older sources are not as good as they might be). Finally, something very important to keep in mind: Just because something is part of folklore doesn't necessarily mean it's beautiful, admirable, or even morally passable. Folklore is a reflection of culture, and sometimes culture is hella racist and/or sexist, among other disappointing qualities. Fairylore is not exempt from this. We've deliberately edited this collection to avoid especially egregious examples, but do know that if you seek out our direct sources, particularly those from before the mid-twentieth century, you will encounter some pretty unsettling, even horrific, material.

## FAIRIES THEN AND ALWAYS

It seems like fairies are always already about to be gone forever. From as far back as Chaucer, who wrote in 1392 that all the fairies of the land had already vanished due to the influence of the friars, to the earliest folklorists of the late eighteenth century, to now, people have argued that the tradition of fairylore is right on the precipice of being lost forever. And yet, as scholar Carole Silver writes, they "have never quite left despite the rise of the towns, science, factories and changes of religion." And yet, here we are, writing about fairies in the twenty-first century. As the great fairy folklorist Katharine Briggs once wrote, "Rare, tenuous and fragile as it is, the tradition is still there, and lingers on from generation to generation." There is something truly magical in the tradition of fairylore, and we hope you find some of that magic in these pages.

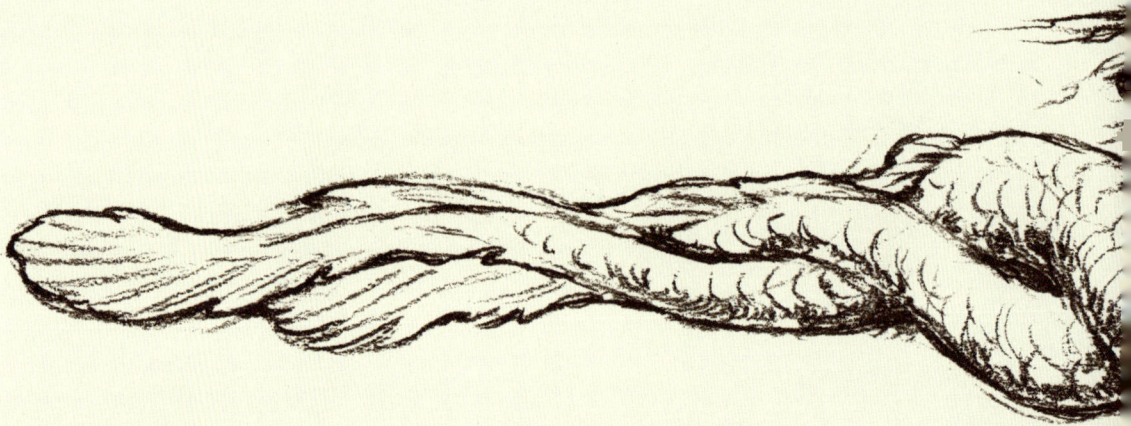

MELUSINE

FRANCE

CHAPTER I

# FAIRIES
*of the*
# HOME

**W**e begin with the fairies of the home: the fairies that literally live inside and closest to us. Fairies of the home are among the most approachable, benevolent, and generally helpful of the bunch. They might help clean, bestow good luck, or offer aid during family emergencies. Some of these fairies are so beloved that people will go through elaborate efforts to attract one to their property, like the Mexican farmers who build little houses and offer gifts of honey to the alux in hopes that one will take up residence!

However, fairies are fairies, so of course some house fairies offer more trouble than they're worth. Norwegian nisses, for example, are useful guardians . . . until they feel disrespected. At that point, you are seriously out of luck because it's *hard* to get rid of a nisse once he's attached to your family, and he is likely to take revenge. And you *really* don't want any Korean moksin tongbŏp to sneak inside because they'll make people sick until they're properly exorcized!

Still, house fairies can be incredibly useful. They can help raise status, offer protection, and act as a bulwark against hardship. In many ways, house fairies help us make sense of what happens in the home, from luck to health to social ties—house fairies externalize these intangible characteristics and make them feel immediate and, possibly, changeable.

# BROWNIE/BOGGART

## UK

The brownie is an "industrious and helpful household spirit" found most commonly in England and the Scottish Lowlands. In older folklore, they loomed human-sized or larger, but more recently, they've appeared "as small, wizened and shaggy, clad in rags or naked." Occasionally, they can take animal forms, and they're "generally grotesque to look at." While brownies frequently have the power of invisibility, they're "so expert in hiding and lurking that they hardly need to exercise it." Incredibly capable and versatile helpers, they take on whatever work needs to be done in or out of the house: "sweeping, churning, spinning, weaving, mowing, thrashing and herding are perhaps the chief." And if they actually like you? They'll take on even more work, up to and including "fetching the midwife."

But, of course, there's always the potential for a sting. While brownies are known for being helpful, they can also be mischievous, even dangerous. This brings us to boggarts, a kind of house fairy poltergeist. The boggart is sometimes considered a sort of cousin to the brownie, but some lore and texts, like "The Lancashire Boggart," suggest brownies can actually become boggarts if you irritate them enough. So, depending on the perspective and text, we might be looking at two different fairy types, or we might be looking at a brownie-boggart continuum.

Katharine Briggs relates this tale of a (sort of?) helpful brownie in Perthshire:

A Brownie on the Celtic fringe, on the edge of the Gaelic-speaking country in Perthshire, haunted Altmor Burn, not far from Pitlochry. He used to be heard paddling and splashing in the burn, then he would go up with wet feet to the farm nearby, and if everything had been left untidy, he would tidy it, but if it was left neat, he would throw everything about. It was counted unlucky to meet him, and the road was avoided at night. He was laid, not by a gift of clothes, but by a nickname. A man returning very merry

from the market one dark night heard him splashing about in the burn, and cried out jovially, "Well, Puddlefoot, how is it with you the night?" The Brownie was horrified. "Oh! Oh!" he cried, "I've gotten a name! 'Tis Puddlefoot they call me!" And he vanished, never to haunt the place again.

# ZASHIKI-WARASHI

## JAPAN

The zashiki-warashi is a house spirit that's especially prevalent in the Tohoku region in northeast Japan and the Iwate Prefecture in particular. As always, there are many regional variations on this creature's name. You can also find him as zashiki bokko, heya bokko, kura warashi, or kome tsuki warashi.

The name "zashiki-warashi" translates as "parlor child" or "little boy of the house," which echoes this creature's physical appearance. He usually takes the shape of a boy child under the age of thirteen, but the zashiki-warashi can occasionally be female, too.

Not all houses are lucky enough to have a zashiki-warashi in residence, but those that do? The families that live in them prosper. Should the zashiki-warashi depart, that luck will evaporate, and the family's fortunes will quickly decline.

Even the residents of the houses where zashiki-warashi live usually don't see this yōkai—instead, they notice the subtle reverberations of his presence, like flipped pillows or strange noises.

Yaganita Kunio relates this story of how a zashiki-warashi's presence was detected in one household:

> The mother of Kizen Sasaski was sewing alone one day when she heard the sound of paper rustling in the next room. That room was only for the master of the house, but he was in Tokyo. Thinking it strange, she opened the door and looked in, but no one was there. Having sat down for a short while, she now heard the sound of someone sniffing in the next room. She concluded that it must be Zashikiwarashi. It has been rumored for some time that Zashikiwarashi resided in this house. A house that this kami (spirit) lives in is said to become rich and prestigious.

While the zashiki-warashi is usually benevolent, there are still sinister possibilities at play. He has a connection to changeling lore, and he may be linked to mabiki, or infanticide.

# BANNIK

## SLAVIC COUNTRIES

Technically the bannik is a spirit of the bathhouse rather than a standard house spirit, but let's roll with it. He's small in stature but very dangerous to humans. The bannik occupies an important social role in Slavic supernatural folklore: "He acts as the intermediary between household spirits and spirits of the forest, field, and stream who come to use the bathhouse for social events." He has another important function, too: punishing those who don't bathe frequently enough!

# KILLMOULIS

## SCOTLAND, UK

The killmoulis is a fairy associated with mills from the Scottish Lowlands. He's extremely protective of his mill and loves to play pranks, which can get a little unruly. He can only be reined in by the intervention of his miller through "direct invocation." Despite being a trickster, he might sometimes help during an emergency, especially at his mill, but he's definitely more of a bother than a helper.

In appearance, he's "a grotesque creature, with an enormous nose and no mouth, though he is said to be very fond of pork." Because he has no mouth, he must inhale his food through his nose, which is quite the picture.

# LUTIN

## FRANCE

The French lutin is a shapeshifter fairy and a troublemaker. They change into different animals to play out their mischief! See a pure white cat? Could be a lutin. They can also turn into a horse conveniently outfitted with a saddle, but we advise against trying to ride them, because they go fast and they'll take you much farther than you ever intended to go. They "play other tricks too, making holes in fishing nets, tangling up people's hair while they sleep, or filling their shoes with stones." You can get rid of these troublesome guys with salt. Like many fairy creatures, they can't step over it.

Fun fact: Famed fairy-tale author Madame D'Aulnoy has a story called "Prince Lutin."

# ALUX

## MEXICO

The alux is a small fairy from Mayan folklore of the Yucatan Peninsula. More specifically, "The Alux is a dominant oral character among the Yucatec Maya and is spoken of mainly in villages such as San Antonio and San Jose Succotz, in the Cayo District. Oral stories of the Alux are also told at Ambergris Caye on the coast of Belize." The alux might also be called duendecillo or "Donato and his brothers." He stands about a foot high, though he has the appearance of a full-grown Maya.

The alux dwells deep in nature, especially the jungles and forests, but a determined farmer could entice them onto a farm. The best strategy for this is to build a miniature house for them to live in and to provide gifts of the harvest, like corn and honey. If the farmer is successful and an alux takes up residence, he'll bring good luck, good weather, and protection from intruders. However, this bounty has an expiration date of seven years, at which point the farmer must close up the house and say goodbye. If he doesn't, the alux will turn on the farmer and bestow bad luck on him!

The alux "serves a social function within the village; it is the reminder of the past tied together with the present and the daily struggle to work the land. Each variation of the Alux is the interpretation of the storyteller as he or she weaves the tapestry of life in the Belizean River Valley and the daily interaction with the land."

Interestingly, Fredy Rodríguez-Mejía and James D. Sexton note that "it cannot be ascertained whether or not the aluxes existed prior to the conquest period." Sometimes they get confused/merged with beliefs about the Spanish duende as well.

# MOKSIN TONGBŎP

## KOREA

"House fairy" has certain connotations: helpful, domestic, maybe unobtrusive. And then there's the moksin tongbŏp. They're pretty much the opposite of helpful, preferring instead to sneak into human houses and inflict mysterious illnesses on the inhabitants within. Luckily, they can't waltz right in. Instead, they have to try to infiltrate a house by hiding inside firewood, furniture, or other wooden objects that the inhabitants are carrying indoors! In a sense, they have to be "invited" (okay, carried) in to cross the threshold of the home, which feels more than a smidge vampiric to us.

Laurel Kendall explains that wood imps (nangu moksin) and earth imps (chisin tongbŏp) can be disturbed when a household member attracts their attention by doing something too dangerous, unlucky, or taboo. A story she collected places the blame for illness and infestation squarely on firewood. Her informant told her,

> "My mother-in-law was sick last year so we did an exorcism. She had a headache and ached in her arms and legs. The *mansin* said it was because of some wood they brought in and stored under the porch." A *mansin* is a kind of supernatural doctor who determines the cause of a supernatural ailment and offers a treatment through ritual to exorcize the offending spirits. However, "the *mansin*'s work is not complete until she burns moxa to fumigate the whole house and catches the imps in a bubbling caldron. Otherwise, infection persists in the body of the house and someone else may fall victim to the troublesome imps. As a precaution against further infestation, the *mansin* pastes charms on the vulnerable spots and secures the house boundaries."

Another story collected by Kendall shows the moksin tongbŏp physically causing illness as well as the treatment that banishes them:

A Cho man suffered from a nagging and congested chest. During the Cho family *kut*, the *mansin*'s visions revealed wood imps clinging to the Cho man's chest. On the final morning of the *kut*, a *mansin* burned moxa and red pepper around the base of the newly constructed toilet shed and along the wood pile.

Bottom line? You don't want these guys in your house.

# HALTIJA

## FINLAND

Haltijas, which translates to "holders," includes a wide range of Finnish folkloric creatures that protect the natural world and some human places like farms. Sometimes even trees have their own special haltija guardian. Traditionally, Finnish families had a haltijapuu, or fairy tree, in their garden. On significant days and special occasions, "the old custom is to leave food and gifts under the tree for the haltija who lives there, to thank it for guarding the household." There's also a tradition in which every individual has their own personal haltija who watches over them.

# DUENDE

## IBERIA AND SOUTH AMERICA

Duendes are mischievous, gnomelike creatures from the folklore of Iberia and parts of South America. They favor big, pointed hats, and some accounts report that they don't have thumbs. It's said that duendes can take "the form of a boy doll or a little man who hops and jumps" and that they may be a demon or even the devil in disguise. While the forests are their natural habitat, they might come into human homes, where "they hide in the walls and jump out to scare children, or make objects go missing." If a duende gets inside, their mischief can be easily mitigated—simply give them the first bit of your food, thrown over your shoulder so that they can scoop it up undetected.

The duende are likely both Hispanic and Mayan in origin, and they overlap with the alux, which, as we mentioned earlier, are sometimes called by the same name. Spanish conquerors may have brought over the concept of the duende, leading to the development of the alux, or at least merging with an existing concept, but from this distance in time and under the impact of colonialism, it's impossible to parse with certainty.

# MAZZAMURELLO

## ITALY

A mazzamurello is usually a creature of the forest, but sometimes they like to move into people's homes! It's said that you might have one living with you if you hear "knocking and banging" on your walls. This clamoring noise is supposed to communicate information to the humans of the household—"either there is a hidden treasure somewhere on the property, or someone in the house is in great danger."

Fun fact: There's a wine named after this fairy that comes from the same region he tends to be found—the Abruzzo region of Italy.

# SACI PERERÊ

## BRAZIL

The saci pererê is a one-legged fairy from Brazil that likes to cause mischief. If something goes wrong around the house, like a pot boiling over, a saci pererê might get the blame! He also likes trailing people in the forest, whistling as he goes, and he can move with great alacrity. A saci pererê has the power of invisibility, which can result in the whimsical sight of his bright red cap bobbing along, seemingly independently, through the trees. Should "you manage to snatch the cap, he must grant you a wish—but this is not as good as it sounds. The cap smells terrible, and you'll never wash the stink away!" You can evade him through traditional methods like crossing running water or dropping a piece of string that's been tied in knots, which he will have to stop and untangle before proceeding.

# DVOROVOI

## SLAVIC COUNTRIES

A dvorovoi (or dvorovyk or domovoy) is the spirit of the farmyard or court-yard, and he's sometimes mixed up with the domovoi or spirit of the house. He oversees all the buildings on the farmstead around the house but not the house itself, which is outside his domain. His role is to protect the farm animals that live in those buildings and around his farm. "When purchasing a new farm animal, it is important to select one of the color that the dvorovoi/domovoi likes." He tends to be solitary in nature.

# KOBOLD

## GERMANY

The kobold are German household spirits. "Kobold" can be used generically to refer to fairies in general, but it can also mean something a lot more specific. This particular fairy is child-sized but with the features of an adult, though he is pretty universally described as "hideous in appearance." He often has "a big head with strong, projecting nose, long, thin arms and bandy legs that seem too weak to support his corpulent frame, and rough, sometimes red, hair that almost obscures his small grey eyes. He looks like a wrinkled old man." He is often black or gray in color and "wear[s] Old Frankish peasant dress, or red stockings and a long grey, green or red jacket, or a green suit, white stockings and buckled shoes and so forth. He also appears dressed as a friar." Delightfully, every kobold has in their possession a hat that grants him the power of invisibility. These hats range in size and color, from white nightcap to red pointed bonnet.

Their temperaments are notoriously surly—they're easily annoyed, cannot be trusted, and enjoy teasing and tormenting. The best part of their nature comes out when they're around horses, which they love. However, when a kobold is irritated or neglected, he "behaves like a poltergeist; his revenge can be fatal."

# NISSE

## SCANDINAVIA

The nisse is the Norwegian and Danish version of a fairy that is extremely common throughout Scandinavian folklore. Other names include tomte (Sweden), tomtenisse and tonttu (Finland). "Nisse" is sometimes translated into English as "brownie," "goblin," or "hobgoblin," but he's really his own thing. A nisse tends to be short in stature, with a long white or gray beard, and a distinctive, brightly colored hat. He loves porridge (there's a widespread folk belief about giving your nisse porridge once a year) and horses (to pet, not eat). The nisse is especially delighted by moonlight, and in the winter months he enjoys playing outside and riding in sledges.

Living inside human dwellings, usually houses and barns, the nisse functions as a guardian. If a nisse is treated kindly, he will protect the household and its livestock, increase prosperity, and possibly help with household labor. However, he is temperamental and easily insulted. If he thinks he's not being properly treated, he will menace his household, playing tricks, stealing valuables, and possibly harming the family's livestock. And you *really* don't want your nisse to be mad at you because it is apparently extremely difficult to get rid of a nisse once he's attached to a household. There are stories of families moving to get away from a nisse that they've displeased, only to find the nisse hidden among their boxes and bags, packed and ready to move along with the departing family!

While the nisse has long been popular in Scandinavian folklore, especially after the rise of Romanticism in the nineteenth century and the recognition of cultural heritage as a kind of national resource, he's become increasingly famous. In more recent times, he's been associated with the winter, especially Christmas and the winter solstice. He has featured in Scandinavian literature, including the work of famed folklorists Peter Christen Asbjørnsen and Jørgen Engebretsen Moe, and in the work of Hans Christian Andersen. In 1852, Andersen published "The Goblin and the Grocer," or "Nissen hos Spekhøkeren" in Danish, a story about a nisse who learns to value both

poetry and Christmas culinary treats. The grocer ensures the nisse's loyalty by giving him "a dish of jam with a large lump of butter in the middle." This story was edited by Andrew Lang and included in his *Pink Fairy Book* in 1897, and you can read it at the end of this chapter.

# THE BEAN-TIGHE

## IRELAND[ISH]

The bean-tighe is known as "the fairy housekeeper of the enchanted submerged castle of the Earl of Desmond," which is about the best job description we've ever heard. She is "supposed to appear sitting on an ancient earthen monument shaped like a great chair and hence called *Suidheachan*, the 'Housekeeper's Little Seat,' on Knock Adoon (Hill of the Fort), which juts out into the Lough."

Sounds great, right? Well, this one is a little more complicated. Evans-Wentz is the oldest source that we can find referencing a fairy called a "bean-tighe," and his book is from 1911. There's also the fact that "bean-tighe" literally just means "'woman of the house' or 'housekeeper' and is used in modern Irish with absolutely no fairy connotations." When we looked more closely at Evans-Wentz's writing on the bean-tighe, a footnote suggested this story was actually about the bean sidhe, as did the inclusion of a golden comb in the story. (Bean sidhe are often associated with combs in Irish folklore.) As folklorist Morgan Daimler argues, "It seems clear that the passage was not meant to refer to a fairy called a 'bean-tighe' but to a fairy bean tighe, or fairy housekeeper" (in other words, to a housekeeper who happened to also be a fairy), and that a "bean-tighe" is not actually a distinct fairy of Irish fairylore at all. Despite this, discussion of the bean-tighe as a kind of fairy—one who cleans the home, watches over children, and loves strawberries with cream—has proliferated online and even in some books. And much of this new invention seems to be driven by non-Irish creators. So, if you see a reference to the bean-tighe, now you know!

What the GOBLIN saw in the Student's room

AN ILLUSTRATION BY H.J. FORD FOR *THE PINK FAIRY BOOK*
BY ANDREW LANG, FROM 1897

# The Goblin and the Grocer

*By Hans Christian Andersen*
*Edited by Andrew Lang*

## DENMARK

"The Goblin and the Grocer" is a tale by Hans Christian Andersen—yes,
of fairy-tale fame! Originally the word "goblin" in the title was "nissen."
W. A. Craigie, who translated the story for inclusion in Andrew Lang's
*The Pink Fairy Book*, chose the word "goblin," so we have left that intact
here (though we would argue that a "nisse" and a "goblin"
are two very different things!).

There was once a hard-working student who lived in an attic, and he had nothing in the world of his own. There was also a hard-working grocer who lived on the first floor, and he had the whole house for his own.

The Goblin belonged to him, for every Christmas Eve there was waiting for him at the grocer's a dish of jam with a large lump of butter in the middle.

The grocer could afford this, so the Goblin stayed in the grocer's shop; and this teaches us a good deal. One evening the student came in by the back door to buy a candle and some cheese; he had no one to send, so he came himself.

He got what he wanted, paid for it, and nodded a good evening to the grocer and his wife (she was a woman who could do more than nod; she could talk).

When the student had said good night he suddenly stood still, reading the sheet of paper in which the cheese had been wrapped.

It was a leaf torn out of an old book—a book of poetry.

"There's more of that over there!" said the grocer. "I gave an old woman some coffee for the book. If you like to give me twopence you can have the rest."

"Yes," said the student, "give me the book instead of the cheese. I can eat my bread without cheese. It would be a shame to leave the book to be torn up. You are a clever and practical man, but about poetry you understand as much as that old tub over there!"

And that sounded rude as far as the tub was concerned, but the grocer laughed, and so did the student. It was only said in fun.

But the Goblin was angry that anyone should dare to say such a thing to a grocer who owned the house and sold the best butter.

When it was night and the shop was shut, and everyone was in bed except the student, the Goblin went upstairs and took the grocer's wife's tongue. She did not use it when she was asleep, and on whatever object in the room he put it that thing began to speak, and spoke out its thoughts and feelings just as well as the lady to whom it belonged. But only one thing at a time could use it, and that was a good thing, or they would have all spoken together.

The Goblin laid the tongue on the tub in which were the old newspapers.

"Is it true," he asked, "that you know nothing about poetry?"

"Certainly not!" answered the tub. "Poetry is something that is in the papers, and that is frequently cut out. I have a great deal more in me than the student has, and yet I am only a small tub in the grocer's shop."

And the Goblin put the tongue on the coffee-mill, and how it began to grind! He put it on the butter-cask, and on the till, and all were of the same opinion as the waste-paper tub, and one must believe the majority.

"Now I will tell the student!" and with these words he crept softly up the stairs to the attic where the student lived.

There was a light burning, and the Goblin peeped through the key-hole and saw that he was reading the torn book that he had bought in the shop.

But how bright it was! Out of the book shot a streak of light which grew into a large tree and spread its branches far above the student. Every leaf was alive, and every flower was a beautiful girl's head, some with dark and shining eyes, others with wonderful blue ones. Every fruit was a glittering star, and there was a marvellous music in the student's room. The little Goblin had never even dreamt of such a splendid sight, much less seen it.

He stood on tiptoe gazing and gazing, till the candle in the attic was put out; the student had blown it out and had gone to bed, but the Goblin remained standing outside listening to the music, which very softly and sweetly was now singing the student a lullaby.

"I have never seen anything like this!" said the Goblin. "I never expected this! I must stay with the student."

The little fellow thought it over, for he was a sensible Goblin. Then he sighed, "The student has no jam!"

And on that he went down to the grocer again. And it was a good thing that he did go back, for the tub had nearly worn out the tongue. It had read everything that was inside it, on the one side, and was just going to turn itself round and read from the other side when the Goblin came in and returned the tongue to its owner.

But the whole shop, from the till down to the shavings, from that night changed their opinion of the tub, and they looked up to it, and had such faith in it that they were under the impression that when the grocer read the art and drama critiques out of the paper in the evenings, it all came from the tub.

But the Goblin could no longer sit quietly listening to the wisdom and intellect downstairs. No, as soon as the light shone in the evening from the attic it seemed to him as though its beams were strong ropes dragging him up, and he had to go and peep through the key-hole. There he felt the sort of feeling we have looking at the great rolling sea in a storm, and he burst into tears. He could not himself say why he wept, but in spite of his tears he felt quite happy. How beautiful it must be to sit under that tree with the student, but that he could not do; he had to content himself with the key-hole and be happy there!

There he stood out on the cold landing, the autumn wind blowing through the cracks of the floor. It was cold—very cold, but he first found it out when the light in the attic was put out and the music in the wood died away. Ah! then it froze him, and he crept down again into his warm corner; there it was comfortable and cosy.

When Christmas came, and with it the jam with the large lump of butter, ah! then the grocer was first with him.

But in the middle of the night the Goblin awoke, hearing a great noise and knocking against the shutters—people hammering from outside. The watchman was blowing his horn: a great fire had broken out; the whole town was in flames.

Was it in the house? or was it at a neighbour's? Where was it?

The alarm increased. The grocer's wife was so terrified that she took her gold earrings out of her ears and put them in her pocket in order to save something. The grocer seized his account books, and the maid her black silk dress.

Everyone wanted to save his most valuable possession; so did the Goblin, and in a few leaps he was up the stairs and in the student's room. He was standing quietly by the open window looking at the fire that was burning in the neighbour's house just opposite. The Goblin seized the book lying on the table, put it in his red cap, and clasped it with both hands. The best treasure in the house was saved, and he climbed out on to the roof with it—on to the chimney. There he sat, lighted up by the flames from the burning house opposite, both hands holding tightly on his red cap, in which lay the treasure; and now he knew what his heart really valued most—to whom he really belonged. But when the fire was put out, and the Goblin thought it over—then—

"I will divide myself between the two," he said. "I cannot quite give up the grocer, because of the jam!"

And it is just the same with us. We also cannot quite give up the grocer—because of the jam.

CHAPTER 2

# FAIRIES
*of*
# SEDUCTION

We next turn to the fairies of seduction, the creatures that romance mortals, often with disastrous consequences. Many fairy lovers do care for their mortal companions, but even these tales usually end tragically. Again and again, mortals fail to follow fairy rules, grow homesick, or age faster than their fairy companion. Falling in love with magic is a dangerous business! On the more sinister end of the magically amorous spectrum, fairies can use seduction for deliberately nefarious purposes. All over the world, there are tales of fairies who pretend to fall in love with mortals in order to drown them, spirit them away, dance them to death, suck their blood, or even drain their life essence! Basically? Mix love and fairies at your own risk.

# LEANNÁN SÍDHE

## IRELAND AND THE ISLE OF MAN

Translated as "fairy mistress" or "fairy sweetheart," the leannán sídhe (or lhiannan-shee on the Isle of Man) is the nightmarish fantasy of the worst possible girlfriend imaginable. Have you ever read about (or, worse, experienced) a partner who seems to suck the life out of her beloved? That's the literal function of the leannán sídhe. She's an irresistible beauty who's definitely going to ruin your life.

If this sounds a little vampiric to you, you're not wrong. Though she doesn't usually feed on blood, she does require a different kind of life force.

In Irish and Manx lore, the leannán sídhe is most likely to pick out a struggling artist in need of inspiration. In exchange for providing the artist with the will and creative force to make the best art of his life, the leannán sídhe siphons away his life energy, and his body fails. The artist will create masterpieces, but his time to make them will run very short once the leannán sídhe strikes her bargain.

W. B. Yeats describes this dynamic in his *Fairy and Folk Tales of the Irish Peasantry*:

> The Leanhaun Shee (fairy mistress), seeks the love of mortals. If
> they refuse, she must be their slave; if they consent, they are hers,
> and can only escape by finding another to take their place. The
> fairy lives on their life, and they waste away. Death is no escape
> from her. She is the Gaelic muse, for she gives inspiration to those
> she persecutes. The Gaelic poets die young, for she is restless, and
> will not let them remain long on earth—this malignant phantom.

Not all takes on the leannán sídhe are equally severe. Lady Wilde, in her *Ancient Legends of Ireland*, writes that "the Leanan-Sidhe, or the spirit of life, was supposed to be the inspirer of the poet and singer, as the Ban-Sidhe was the spirit of death, the foreteller of doom," suggesting a much more benevolent role.

Whether we follow Yeats's more sinister take or Wilde's pure muse, tales of the leannán sídhe always hinge on a fairy obsession with human art. As we mentioned in our introduction, Celtic fairies have a history of fascination with human crafts and seem to be largely unable to make equivalent creations themselves. These fairies covet human art to the point that many victims of fairy kidnappings were great artists in some way, stolen away to fairyland to entertain their fairy captors.

The leannán sídhe remains a gamble: Art and inspiration, but at what cost? Would you invite her in or cut and run?

Fun fact: There is another Irish fairy, the baobhan sith, who initially seems very similar to the leannán sídhe . . . buuuuut she actually does the whole bloodsucking thing. Given that *Dracula* (1897) was written by an Irish man, Bram Stoker, we're pretty sure that there's more than a little fairy inspiration in the idea of the vampire as we know him today.

# VILA

## SLAVIC COUNTRIES

The Slavic vila is another fairy you probably don't want to date. Under a variety of names, she can be found in Bulgaria, the Czech Republic, Poland, and other nearby regions. In the Czech tradition, and some others, vile are extremely beautiful, dangerous women with long hair. They are able to entrance and seduce unwary men who cross their paths and intrude on their land—they do not like to be watched and are not hesitant to express that displeasure. Their beauty, voices, and dances are often used to lure men to their destruction. Despite their deadliness, they're largely ambivalent toward humans. In fact, in legends and fairy tales, vile may help or hinder a hero. They're just as likely to offer aid as they are to kill people or deliberately destroy a harvest. Some stories even depict them as warriors or as benevolent helpers, with healing abilities and kindly dispositions. According to folklorist Natalie Kononenko, a vila was said to have befriended the Serbian hero Marko Kraljevic, who became a notoriously successful warrior himself—supposedly due to this friendship.

Show vile disrespect, however, and they'll start plotting revenge. There are even stories of vile who dip into changeling lore, stealing human children and leaving a fairy or another placeholder behind. To stay on their good side, people sometimes offer them flowers and food.

Vile have close ties to the natural world, and they're associated with forests, the air, and water. Sometimes, they're said to be shapeshifters, with the ability to take the form of birds, horses, wolves, or even whirlwinds. Other tales depict them controlling the wind and making plants grow, a talent that makes the places where they dwell and dance especially lush.

But it's the dancing you need to be wary of.

The nastier vile have a habit of seducing men by inviting them to join a circle dance. Some men do manage to survive the dance and prosper, but more often, they are literally danced to death. It's one of those magical compulsions that's almost impossible to shake.

Like many other fairies, vile toe the line of the living and the dead. In some regions, they're the restless souls of girls who have suffered an early

death. It is this aspect of the vila that features in Adolphe Adam's ballet *Giselle*, first performed in 1841. In his story, vile are the ghosts of the young girls betrayed by their loves. They dance in the moonlit forest, enacting their revenge by dancing young men to death. In some traditions, they're even portrayed as vampire-like: dead women unable to rest in their graves.

# FOX SPIRITS

## JAPAN, CHINA, KOREA, AND VIETNAM

Numerous Asian countries have folklore about fox spirits, creatures that can transform into beautiful women in order to seduce blissfully unaware mortal men. Sometimes, these fox spirits are genuinely in love with their chosen mortals . . . but sometimes, they really just want to eat their heart or liver, so proceed with caution. Called the kitsune in Japan, the hulijing in China, the kumiho in Korea, and the hồ ly tinh in Vietnam, they're all a little different, but many of the basic characteristics remain surprisingly stable. For example, across cultures, they often have very long lives, multiple tails, and a lot of energy.

Many of the stories about these Asian fox fairies seem to have roots in the hulijing of China. In fact, as sinologist and translator John Minford points out, "these shapeshifting, irresistibly beautiful 'were-vixen' [. . .] ha[ve] haunted the Chinese male imagination for centuries." It's here that we first see the strange duality of these creatures. They're very seductive, and they can be "destructive and heartless, ruthless and vindictive," even to the point where some tales say they suck life force out of men in a similar fashion to the leannán sídhe of Ireland. But other stories tell of their intense loyalty and love. Minford believes that this reflects the general attitude of men toward women in China at the time these stories circulated. The hulijing were attractive but dangerous, and it was believed that their yin (feminine) energy could overtake the men's yang (masculine) energy, even to the point of possession, a preoccupation that provoked "a lethal mixture of infatuation, fascination, and fear." Honestly, it's not dissimilar to the idea we have today of a guy being too "whipped" by his girlfriend—the perceived danger of surrendering masculine power in favor of love. Moving that danger away from actual women and to a supernatural entity, however, both diminishes it and reinforces the helplessness of men in the face of such power. ("It's magic, bro! You couldn't have resisted! You're totally still manly!")

These stories clearly influenced the other tales of Asian fox spirits. The kitsune, for example, is one of the most famous yōkai in Japan, but she's one of the most common Japanese folkloric creatures to hear about *outside* of Japan, too. In fact, at this point, she's much more well known internationally than the hulijing, who likely inspired her. The reason for this is that she really does pop up in a lot of different places—Japanese folklore, of course, but also historical records, literary texts, theater productions, and, nowadays, pop culture, including manga and anime. She actually goes by several different names according to region, but "kitsune" is the most common word you'll encounter to describe her.

In the earliest Japanese texts, kitsune tend to be omens, sometimes good and sometimes bad, but the stories about them transforming into beautiful women are very old, too—ninth-century old, at least. As in China, you get stories where the fox spirits are dangerous and not to be messed with, and there are numerous tales of fox possession or bewitching. In the possession tales, the fox spirit actually takes over a human's body. They do this to deliver an important message, obtain resources, or simply to make some serious mischief. Possession might also occur because the fox actually wants to *help* the human, usually because the hapless mortal is in some kind of danger.

There are also, of course, romantic stories in the Japanese tradition as well. In a collection of old Buddhist legends translated into English by Kyoko Motomochi Nakamura and called *Miraculous Stories from the Japanese Buddhist Tradition*, there is a story about a man who encounters a beautiful, energetic girl and marries her. They eventually have a son, and, around the same time, their pet dog has a puppy. The puppy barks at the wife all the time, and one day, the wife is so startled by the barking that she suddenly transforms into a fox and hops on top of a nearby hedge to get away from it. The couple is eventually forced to separate, but their love endures. The wife returns every night to her husband, and the text explains that this is where the word "kitsune" comes from: "kitsu," which means "to come," and "ne," which is the word for "sleep." According to folklorist Michael Dylan Foster, this etymology isn't likely accurate, but it's a delightful bit of folklore. These stories of devoted fox wives can be found throughout Japanese cultural texts as much as the tales that paint them in a more negative light.

It's worth noting that the kitsune of Japan are also frequently connected to the worship of Inari, the kami, or god, of rice fields, farming, fertility, warfare, and even prostitution. Inari worship has likely been present since the Nara period of Japan's history, but foxes were not associated with it until the eleventh century at the earliest. In this understanding of the fairy, the kitsune is not the Inari deity itself. Instead, the fox is the messenger or attendant of the deity. This is why fox statues are placed in front of Inari shrines throughout Japan. As Foster points out, though, there isn't really a 100 percent straightforward connection between kitsune and Inari worship. They definitely "overlap and mutually influence each other, if not in religious doctrine then certainly in the popular imagination," but they're not quite the same thing either.

In Korea, the kumiho is much more on the dangerous side of the equation. You're less likely to find love stories or stories of fae kindness featuring fox spirits in all but the oldest Korean folklore. There's seduction, yes, but it seems to typically be in pursuit of devouring human livers or hearts or the whole body and soul, so maybe don't bring her home. For example, in the Korean folktale "The Fox Sister," an older couple has several sons, but wants a daughter so much that they pray for one, saying that they would love and accept her even if she was a fox. If you know anything about fairy tales, you know that you should *never* make wishes like this, because you never know who might be listening or what their sense of humor is like. The couple is granted a daughter, but she turns out to indeed be a fox spirit, whose appetite grows each day until she winds up eating her parents and one of her brothers. Different versions of the story feature different methods the other brothers use to defeat her, but this is definitely the kind of fox fairy we're generally dealing with in Korea. Some of these stories say that a fox spirit must eat a certain number of humans before she can become human herself; others say that if she falls in love and can refrain from eating that person for a thousand days, then she can also become human, but we're not sure the risk is worth it. Less seems to be known about the Vietnamese hồly tinh, but she's definitely a similar, shapeshifting creature with multiple tails.

A dangerous shapeshifter, a creature capable of possession, a romantic Other, a local deity, and more—fox spirits *really* can't be contained to representing just one function as far as fairies go. We've chosen to put her with the other fairies of seduction, as the stories of their love—and their vengeance—are delightfully haunting and memorable.

# TAMAWO

## PHILIPPINES

Based on the stories we've told you so far, it might seem like the most seductive fairies tend to be female—after all, so far we've told you about female fairies who trade inspiration for life force, those who dance their would-be lovers to death, and fox spirits who transform into beautiful women. But a certain kind of the tamawo of the Philippines are male . . . and just as dangerous.

According to Filipino folklore, these specific tamawo are human-sized, mostly male fairies who live in a mostly invisible parallel world. However, they really like coming over into our world and luring human women back to their realms to be their wives. Anna Claybourne describes the tamawo as "handsome with pale, glowing skin, hair, and eyes. They wear a golden crown and have golden fangs and claws."

Here's a little taste of their MO: Scholar Barbara Jean Sibley describes a story in which a young girl was approached by a man at a dance, who told her that he "came here only to visit you." When he vanished, she waited for him, but grew sick almost immediately after. When she was brought to a folk healer, "she said that the man [with] whom I dance[d] is not a real human being like us, but he is different from us, in other words he is a tamao [Sibley's spelling]. She said that this tamao is in love with me." Sibley's informant told her that she saw the man again later, and that he was "very handsome, tall, white complexion, with curly hair." He took her to a beautiful house and even introduced her to his parents! He wanted her to take off her Catholic medallion and eat his food, both of which she refused, which made him run away. After that, she realized she was not in a beautiful house, but rather "sitting in a jackfruit tree." Later, the tamawo told her that he had to go away for a while because he was going to be "studying [medicine] in France"—yes, *seriously*! It sounds to us like he decided she was too much trouble to kidnap, so he made up an excuse to ghost her. ("I can't, I have to go study medicine in France" is the best excuse we've ever heard. Use it freely.)

Now, the seductive male tamawo is just one kind of Filipino tamawo. Others are more on the mischievous side, fairies who can shapeshift into different animals. (Pro tip: If you look closely, you can always tell. For one thing, the animal's toes are always too long and their claws *way* too big!) They can try the kidnapping move with children, too, which W. H. Millington and Berton L. Maxfield say they do in order to make the children into creatures like themselves. To accomplish this, they must make the child eat some of the food of their world, but if the child can "successfully resis[t] them, the child is, at the end of three or four days, taken back to the spot where he was captured, and released." Our takeaway: Tamawo really enjoy kidnapping humans, but only when it's easy.

For a deeper look at what happens when you break a taboo set by a fairy wife, one of the best examples is the French story "Melusine." This legend is very old, possibly with roots in Scotland, but the best-known French version goes something like this: Once upon a time, there was a king who fell in love with a beautiful fountain fairy named Pressine. They married and had three daughters, Melusine, Melior, and Palatine, but Pressine made her husband promise he would never visit her "in her lyings-in," as folklorist William Thomas puts it. When he found out about the daughters, he rushed to Pressine's chambers and burst in while she was bathing them. Furious that he had broken his word, Pressine took the three girls and disappeared.

Many years later, Melusine asked her mother why she had left their father, and when told he had broken a promise and that otherwise they would have been living happily with him in his palace, Melusine vowed revenge. Ultimately, she and her sisters imprisoned her father in a mountain, but her mother was not on board. She cast a spell on Melusine as punishment, decreeing that she would transform into a snake from the waist down every Saturday. The curse could only be broken if she met a man who would marry her under the condition of never seeing her on Saturday . . . and keep that promise.

Sometime later, Melusine fell in love with a man named Raymond, who agreed to her condition that he never see her on Saturday. At first he kept his promise faithfully, but eventually, things went to pieces. A cousin convinced Raymond that Melusine must be spending Saturdays with a lover, because why else would she make such a weird demand of him? Consumed by jealousy, he hid himself and saw Melusine in her half-snake form. He instantly realized what he had done, but it was too late. Melusine was forced to leave him, and they both spent the rest of their days in anguish for all that they had lost.

Melusine and Raymond's tragic story has inspired numerous works, from Letitia Landon's nineteenth-century poem "The Fairy of the Fountains," to A. S. Byatt's famous novel *Possession*, to musical versions of the story like those by Sharon Knight and Nolwenn Leroy.

MELUSINE

# APSARA

## INDIA

Apsaras are celestial beings that appear in Hindu and Buddhist folklore and literature. They're extremely beautiful, shapeshifting women who frequently have relationships with humans, though they're usually associated with the god Indra's court. In fact, they're often sent down to earth explicitly to seduce meditating rishis and distract them from attaining more powers. Otherwise, they tend to marry demigod musicians called gandharvas. They're all about music and dancing, and, nymphlike, they're often tied to the element of water. According to the *Ramayana*, they come from water itself: "Then as the waters foamed and boiled, / As churning still the Immortals toiled, / Of winning face and lovely frame, / Forth sixty million fair ones came. / Born of the foam and water, these / Were aptly named Apsarases."

Apsaras are frequent features of Southeast Asian art, especially sculpture and painting.

# NIKUSUI

## JAPAN

We're returning to Japan once more in this chapter because the nikusui is too weird to omit. The nikusui is said to be a notably vampiric yōkai, but she's kind of hard to find information on in English. Why? Well, it's at least partially because "nikusui" is also the name of a popular Japanese soup! "Nikusui" quite literally means "meat" plus "sip/suck," so it's pretty easy to see how that might be a good name for a soup . . . but it could also easily be translated as "meat sucker," which is terrifying in a fairy-lore context!

Here's what we do know about this mysterious yōkai. Stories about her go back to at least the late 1700s, as she appears in the *Hyakkiyakou—Bakemonogatari*, a book of monsters published in 1785, and there is even a drawing of her from 1802 in a book published by Iseya Jisuke. She sucks flesh from people's bones, not blood, but is otherwise fairly vampire-like in nature. According to Josh Furr, the "Nikusui is a femme-fatal [sic] with the appearance of a voluptuous young woman" who is "known for targeting men walking the mountain roads of the Mie and Wakayama Prefectures late at night." Furr adds that "according to famed author and Wakayama local, Minakata Kumagusu, Nikusui's modus apparatus is to flirtatiously approach a traveling passerby and steal his lantern, asking 'Can I borrow your lamp?,' after which she bites into his flesh, draining it dry." So yeah, don't go handing out flashlights in the Mie and Wakayama Prefectures, okay? We say this for your own safety.

# GWRAGEDD ANNWN

## WALES, UK

According to Katharine Briggs, the Welsh gwragedd annwn "are the nearest thing [British people] have to the classical water nymph." They prefer to live in or near lakes, where they love to sing and play in the water. They row around on the surface in special skiffs and can easily cross between our world and other realms. It's common to hear stories about these fairies where one gwraig annwn marries a mortal man, but then the man loses her because he refuses to follow the rules. In legends of supernatural marriages, the magical partner often has a very specific request of their partner. These "interdictions" include things like "don't look at me while I'm weaving" and "let me bathe alone on Saturdays." Almost always, the man becomes worried or obsessive and eventually does the exact opposite of her wishes. When this happens, he usually loses his enchanted wife forever. It is said that the gwragedd annwn were wildly wealthy (they owned tons of lovely fairy cattle, at least), so it's a double blow to these husbands when they break the taboo—they lose their wife *and* all her wealth!

# MORGAN

## FRANCE

In Brittany, France, there is a group of water fairies called morgans who live in underwater palaces where, some say, the mortals they love can magically survive. Breathing and living underwater in a gorgeous palace with your fairy lover sounds pretty nice, right? Well, there seems to be a slight hiccup for the morgans and their search for mortal true love. M. J. Cuillandre, one of W. Y. Evans-Wentz's informants, told him that "the *Morgan* is a fairy eternally young, a virgin seductress whose passion, never satisfied, drives her to despair" because although her magical songs easily draw men to her, "the arms of the fairy clasp only a corpse; for at her touch men die, and it is this which causes the despair of the amorous and inviolate *Morgan*." So, alas, the underwater palace remains theoretically useful rather than achievable in practice.

Some stories link the morgans to the doomed city of Ys, the legendary Breton city that fell beneath the ocean. When the king's daughter Dahut disobeys her father and causes a flood that destroys their city, her dad sacrifices her to the sea (#greatparenting). Therefore, it's sometimes hypothesized that Dahut was the first (and possibly only) morgan.

# TAPAIRU

## COOK ISLANDS

Remember how the Slavic vile liked to dance people to death? A similar creature exists in the folklore of the Cook Islands. The tapairu are said to be beautiful female fairies that live in a magical pool that connects to Avaiki, the spirit world, where their mother—the death goddess Miru—lives. The legend goes that when the moon is bright, they like to come out and dance. According to Anna Claybourne, when they do, they enjoy "enticing young human men to dance with them." All is fun and games until the end of the dance, when "they then drag their unfortunate victims down through the magical waters to the spirit world, where Miru eats them." So much for a second date.

In Germany, a strange and sad story of fairy seduction is tied to a very specific place. On the bank of the Rhine River, close to Sankt Goarshausen, stands a massive rock. The rock, which is about 433 feet high and very steep, has been designated as a UNESCO World Heritage Site, and the Loreley Amphitheatre sits perched at its peak. The rock itself is called the Lorelei, and it has long been the subject of local folklore. For example, some legends tell of dwarves living in caves deep within the rock . . . but others tell of a beautiful woman who perished in the Rhine when her lover proved faithless. Instead of simply dying, she was transformed into a dangerous siren, the Lorelei, who lures fishermen to their doom.

The story became more fixed in 1801 when Clemens Brentano composed a ballad called "Zu Bacharach am Rheine" ("To Bacharach on the Rhine," sometimes translated as simply "Lore Lay"), which was published in his novel *Godwi*. This ballad tells of a beautiful woman named Lore Lay who is betrayed by her love and accused of a magical and deadly ability to bewitch and destroy men. Instead of having her executed, the bishop sends her away to a nunnery. She encounters Lorelei (the rock) on her journey, and she asks her captors for permission to climb it. When she reaches the summit, she thinks she sees her lover in a boat on the river below, and she plummets to her death. From that day forward, the rock echoed with the sound of her name.

Lord Bishop, let me die!
I'm tired of life
'Cause everyone must perish
who sees my eyes!
The eyes are two flames,
My arm a magic wand—
O lay me in the flames
O break my staff!

LORELEI

Over twenty years later, in 1824, Heinrich Heine adapted Brentano's ballad into his immensely popular poem "Die Lorelei" ("The Lorelei"). Heine's version of the story describes a siren named Lorelei who sits on the cliff above the Rhine and combs her lustrous golden hair, distracting the passing sailors with her extraordinary beauty and causing them to wreck on the hazardous rocks below.

> The loveliest young maiden sits
> So beautifully up there,
> Her golden jewelry gleams and glints,
> She combs her golden hair,
> She combs it with a golden brush
> And while she combs she sings;
> The tune is both miraculous
> And overpowering.

In 1837, Heine's poem was set to music by Friedrich Silcher, and the resulting song "Lorelei" became well-known throughout German-speaking Europe. Many other musical versions have been composed since then.

Though the version of Lorelei the character most know today seems mainly to be a literary creation of Brentano that was subsequently adapted by other creators, the Lorelei has undeniably moved into German popular culture and folklore, appearing in comics, symphonies, and songs by Eagle-Eye Cherry, Styx, George Gershwin, Blackmore's Night, and many others. For an excellent literary take (that also draws on the "Tam Lin" ballad), check out Patricia C. Wrede's short story "The Lorelei."

# RUSALKA

## SLAVIC COUNTRIES

The rusalka is the Slavic aquatic sister to the vila of the forest. Most of the time, rusalki are thought to be the spirits of women who died young, usually those who drowned themselves after becoming pregnant outside of marriage and facing abandonment by their families. Other legends that say unbaptized infants and people who die during the week before Trinity Sunday, the Rusalia week, become rusalki, too. Regardless, upon death, they are transformed into a kind of deadly water fairy who dances and sings to seduce men. Once their prey is within reach, however, the rusalki drown them mercilessly.

Though she's usually depicted with human legs, she's commonly thought of as kin to the mermaid (probably because of the whole singing to and then drowning thing). According to Natalie Kononenko, "[A] *rusalka* typically sits in a tree at night, next to the body of water where she died, combing her hair and singing. Her voice is said to be especially seductive, luring men foolish enough to walk in the forest at night. A *rusalka* who succeeds in getting a man to approach her river or lake pushes him into the water and tickles him to the point at which he cannot swim and drowns." The drive to murder via tickles seems especially cruel—what an awful way to go!

Though the concept of the rusalka is very old, the seduction aspect of her story was likely added later and influenced by written literature. In fact, that mermaid association makes this scenario all the more likely. Kononenko notes that older stories show her as more of a nature fairy, found in all kinds of places rather than exclusively by the water. The tickling thing seems to have always been there, though "*rusalki* were said to tickle both women and men, as well as making crops grow in the places where they had been dancing" —silver lining, we guess?

Special note: In Ukraine there's a very similar creature called the mavka, but she's exclusively bad news. Where she dances, nothing grows at all.

# The Lorelei

*Retold by Lewis Spence*

## GERMANY

We have chosen to give you a story of the Lorelei for
the "Fairies of Seduction" chapter largely because we love
her characterization here! She makes herself seem so
innocent and afraid, only for the illusion to visibly fade
away as she reveals her true power!

Many are the legends which cluster round the name of the Lorelei. In some of the earlier traditions she is represented as an undine, combing her hair on the Loreleiberg and singing bewitching strains wherewith to lure mariners to their death, and one such legend relates how an old soldier named Diether undertook to capture her.

Graf Ludwig, son of the Prince Palatine, had been caught in her toils, his frail barque wrecked, and he himself caught in the whirlpool and drowned. The prince, grievously stricken at the melancholy occurrence, longed to avenge his son's death on the evil enchantress who had wrought such havoc. Among his retainers there was but one who would undertake the venture—a captain of the guard named Diether—and the sole reward he craved was permission to cast the Lorelei into the depths she haunted should he succeed in capturing her.

Diether and his little band of warriors ascended the Lorelei's rock in such a way as to cut off all retreat on the landward side. Just as they reached the summit the moon sailed out from behind a cloud, and behold, the spirit of the whirlpool was seen sitting on the very verge of the precipice, binding her wet hair with a band of gleaming jewels.

"What wouldst thou with me?" she cried, starting to her feet.

"To cast thee into the Rhine, sorceress," said Diether roughly, "where thou hast drowned our prince."

"Nay," returned the maid, "I drowned him not. 'Twas his own folly which cost him his life."

As she stood on the brink of the precipice, her lips smiling, her eyes gleaming softly, her wet dark hair streaming over her shoulders, some strange, unearthly quality in her beauty, a potent spell fell upon the little company, so

PAINTING BY BENJAMIN ULMANN

that even Diether himself could neither move nor speak.

"And wouldst thou cast me in the Rhine, Diether?" she pursued, smiling at the helpless warrior. "'Tis not I who go to the Rhine, but the Rhine that will come to me."

Then loosening the jewelled band from her hair, she flung it on the water and cried aloud: "Father, send me thy white steeds, that I may cross the river in safety."

Instantly, as at her bidding, a wild storm arose, and the river, overflowing its banks, foamed right up to the summit of the Lorelei Rock. Three white-crested waves, resembling three white horses, mounted the steep, and into the hollowed trough behind them the Lorelei stepped as into a chariot, to be whirled out into the stream.

Meanwhile Diether and his companions were almost overwhelmed by the floods, yet they were unable to stir hand or foot. In mid-stream the undine sank beneath the waves: the spell was broken, the waters subsided, and the captain and his men were free to return home.

Nevermore, they vowed, would they seek to capture the Lorelei.

CHAPTER 3

# FAIRIES *of* TERROR

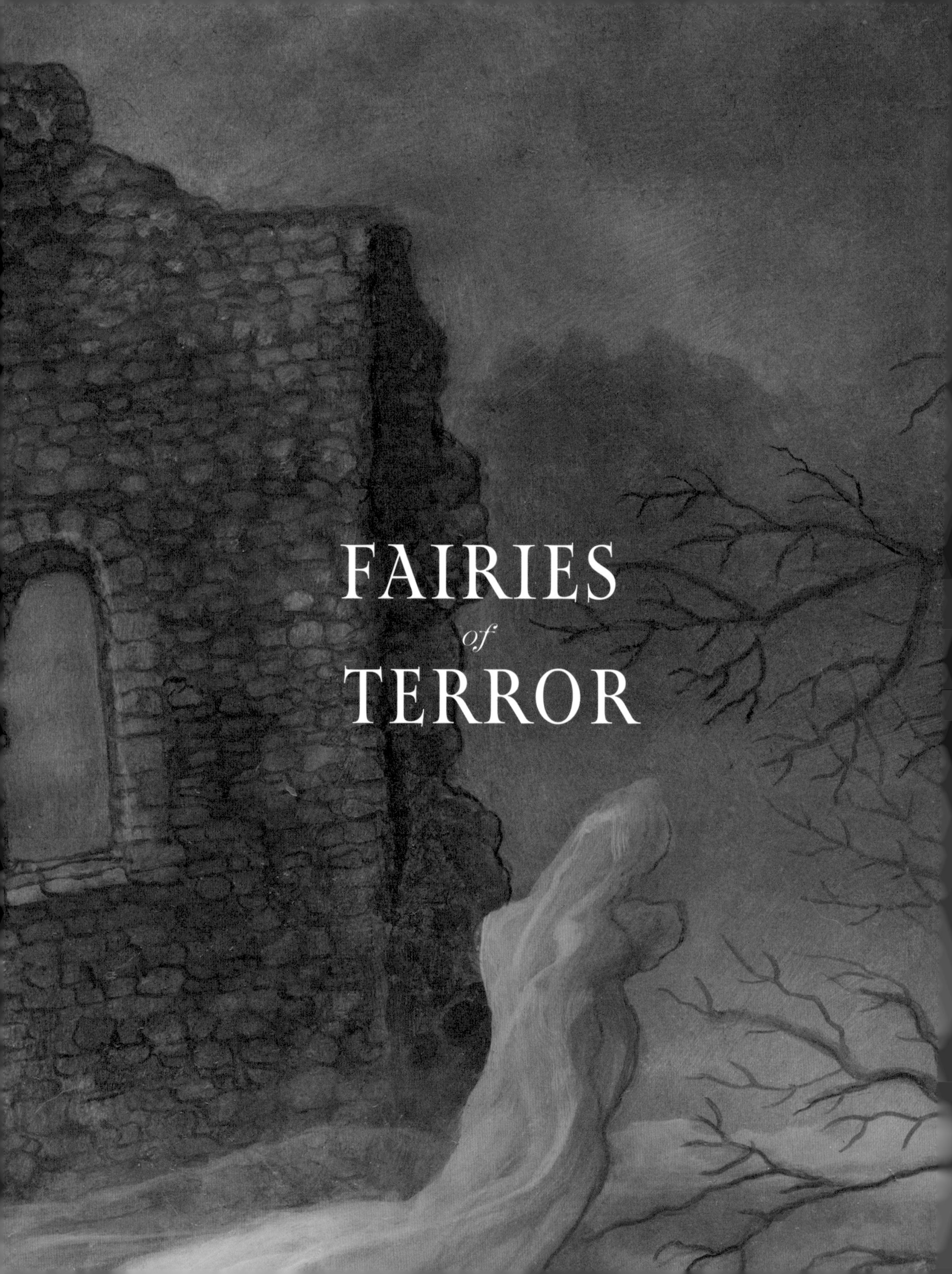

While all fairies have the potential to ruin your day, the fairies gathered in this chapter are among those most likely to ruin—or end—your life. These are the fairies who will gladly kill you just to refresh the red dye on their cute little fairy caps with your blood or chase you down the road while brandishing a whip made from a human spine. Fairies of terror are the closest to death. They represent our deepest fears: existential threats, loss of control of the body, and the inevitability of our lives ending.

While not every single fairy in this chapter is bent on murder—the kamikiri will only cut your hair, after all—they are the most threatening to the integrity of the body and the self, through violation or complete destruction. Read on for a tour of the most sinister side of Faerie.

# ONI

## JAPAN

Oni are one of the vast number of yōkai found throughout Japan, and their name can be translated as demon, devil, or ogre. They're incredibly old yōkai, showing up in documents as early as the eighth century, and while they appear in countless legends and other folk materials, they've successfully migrated into contemporary Japanese media, including manga, anime, and film.

While the physical appearance of the oni has varied widely over its more than 1,200-year history, in recent years, its appearance has really stabilized. Current depictions of the oni usually include one or more of these markers: large size, immense strength, and a humanoid shape. Their faces are dramatic colors (red and blue are especially common), and they often have protruding fangs, horns, and three fingers and toes tipped with sharp claws. They're almost always male, despite female oni definitely appearing in the legendary tradition. They like to carry a staff or club, and they're clothed in a loincloth, or fundoshi, of tiger skin. The horns are probably the most reliable indicator—most oni in contemporary depictions have them.

While not every oni is a baddie—there are stories about comical, harmless, and even helpful oni—the oni is usually intent on human harm. He is usually "a nasty otherworldly being who threatens humans; he is a person-shaped antiperson, encapsulating everything that imperils humans and human society." So basically, oni represent the antithesis of what humans need to survive and thrive.

When we said that oni are an incredibly old part of Japanese folklore, we were not exaggerating. You can find the word "oni" in some of the earliest known Japanese written texts, including the *Kojiki*, *Nihonshoki*, and local histories, or fudoki. Image of oni, or oni-like creatures, are also extremely old and show up in twelfth-century Buddhist hell scrolls (*Jigoku zoshi*). And they're recognizable there, even though the scrolls are eight hundred years old!

Fascinatingly, it seems that oni were once conflated with the whole scope of yōkai, representing a general scary monster, but over time, the oni emerged as its own distinct thing, with specific characteristics: physical characteristics

like horns and fangs, but also things like an affinity for lightning, a terrible temper, and a preferred diet of people.

As their appearance in hell scrolls might suggest, oni can and do represent whatever is currently most threatening and terrifying to humans. In the past, they've represented plague or foreign influence. But they are, at heart, representations of anything that feels too different or unmanageable, anything that culturally feels like an existential threat. For this reason, oni can also potentially represent disruption and rebellion, making the oni doubly powerful as a cultural metaphor.

# DULLAHAN

## IRELAND

On the most basic level, the dullahan is a spectral, headless terror. He likes to travel on horseback, carrying his own grinning head under his arm. His flesh may have the texture of moldy cheese, and he has exceptionally good vision, which is bad news if he decides to chase you down. And, yes, despite clearly being a zombie-adjacent ghost demon, he is firmly considered to be a fairy in Irish tradition.

One of our favorite things about dullahans is their aggressive accessorizing, although in fairness sometimes they're just animated headless corpses without additional paraphernalia. They may, however, carry a whip made from a human spine, drive a wagon covered with human skin, and use human-skull candles.

As you have likely already surmised, the dullahan is strongly associated with death, but not just for aesthetic reasons. Dullahans often appear with extremely ominous horses and carriages, most famously the "death coach." In this capacity, they're often interpreted as omens of death. If a dullahan says your name, legend says you're doomed to die. Of course, if a dullahan is close enough to you for you to hear it say your name, things are probably not looking up for you. Other legends say that dullahans are silent and cannot speak at all. This has led to euphemistically referring to a dullahan as "The Good Woman," ostensibly because the best woman is one who can't talk. Other legends say that if you are foolish enough to open your front door when a dullahan's coach is parked in front of your house, a basin full of blood will be thrown in your face, so that's fun. But in any case, the dullahan appears as a creature whose head has been severed, perhaps one of the most forceful ways to convey loss of life.

In his *Fairy Legends*, Croker describes a gathering of dullahans thusly:

> It was strange music to dance by; nevertheless, moving to it,
> round and round the wheel set with skulls, were well dressed
> ladies and gentlemen, and soldiers and sailors, and priests and

publicans, and jockeys and jennys, but all without their heads. Some poor skeletons, whose bleached bones were ill covered by moth-eaten palls, and who were not admitted into the ring, amused themselves by bowling their brainless noddles at one another, which seemed to enjoy the sport beyond measure.

One of Croker's informants, a man identified as Mr. O'Reilly and the author of an Irish dictionary, offers that "the word Dulachan (in Irish Dubhlachan) signifies a dark, sullen person. The word Durrachan, or Dullahan, by which in some places the goblin is known, has the same signification. It comes from Dorr, or Durr, anger, or Durrach, malicious, fierce, &c." In fairness, Croker himself says this entomology may not be correct, but it's certainly an interesting insight into the folklore if not the literal language.

Croker is far from the only early folklorist to collect material on dulla-hans, but his accounts are *vivid*. We'll leave you with one last description of the dullahan's death coach rushing by:

a great high black coach drawn by six black horses, with long
black tails reaching almost down to the ground, and a coachman
dressed all in black sitting up on the box. But what surprised
Mick the most was, that he could see no sign of a head either
upon coachman or horses. It swept rapidly by him, and he could
perceive the horses raising their feet as if they were in a fine
slinging trot, the coachman touching them up with his long whip,
and the wheels spinning round like hoddy-doddies; still he could
hear no noise.

# REDCAP

## ENGLAND, UK

Redcaps hang out in places that are bad news, especially places with a wicked, bloody past. In British folklore, they're especially thick on the ground in ruined castles along the border between England and Scotland. We might even call them border fairies, fairies that symbolize the tension between two regions.

Katharine Briggs says they live in "towers where dark deeds had been done, and re-dyed their red caps in the blood of travelers who sheltered there." And yes—the most distinctive thing about these fairies, in fact where their name comes from, is that their hats are red because they dye them in human blood. One of the alternative names for them? Bloody caps. These guys are *really* murderous, enabled by their long, sharp teeth, thin fingers tipped with deadly claws, and large eyes. Stumble into a ruin where a redcap lives, and you can look forward to being pelted with rocks until you manage to flee or are killed—in the latter outcome, it's your blood that will be enriching your new friend's hat. You probably can't fight a redcap off physically, but crosses and scripture might cause him to burst into flames, to which we can only say, how delightfully *vampiric*.

Of course, nothing in folklore is ever 100 percent clear-cut, so there are tales of redcaps who bestow good luck. For instance, in the Dutch tradition, red-caps (kaboutermannekins) act more like brownies, benevolent house fairies.

Still, probably best to steer clear of fairies with red caps, just in case they're looking to refresh their color.

# ELOKO

## CONGO RIVER BASIN, AFRICA

An eloko is a small gnomelike creature said to dwell deep in the rainforests surrounding the Congo River. They can look like sweet little nature spirits, and they're sometimes said to be spirits of the local dead, but these guys are, legendarily speaking, very bad news. Biloko (the plural of eloko) are vicious, vengeful creatures with a taste for human flesh and a heavy grudge against humanity in general.

And they do not look it! Biloko live inside tree trunks and dress themselves in leaves. No hair grows on their bodies—instead, they grow grass. However, they also have piercing eyes that glow, sharp claws, and mouths that can, apparently, open wide enough to swallow a human whole! Given these characteristics, biloko carry associations with fertility, growth, death, pythons, and nighttime predators like jackals, civet cats, and lions.

Perhaps the most sinister thing about biloko? They carry little bells, which have the power to charm and ensnare humans who hear them ring. A human who hears this bell is compelled to allow an eloko to *eat them*. Amulets may help to repel this magical effect, but *yikes*.

Here's a story offered by Jan Knappert, a KiSwahili linguist, in his book *African Mythology: An Encyclopedia of Myth and Legend,* that illustrates how deceptively innocent an eloko might appear and how deadly the results of encountering one can be:

> One day a hunter took his wife, at her own insistence, into the forest, where he had a hut with a palisade around it. When he went out to inspect his traps, he told her: "When you hear a bell, do not move. If you do, you will die!" Soon after he had left, she heard the charming sound of a little bell coming closer, for the Biloko have a good nose for feminine flesh. Finally, a gentle voice asked to be let in. It was like the voice of a child. The woman opened the door and there was an *eloko*, smelling like the forest, looking small and innocent. She offered him banana mash with

fried fish but he refused: "We eat only human meat. I have not eaten for a long time. Give me a piece of your arm." At last the woman consented, totally under the spell of the *eloko*. That night, the husband found her bones.

When the wife hears the bell, she *knows* it's a warning but succumbs to the charm. And though she treats the eloko as a respected guest, there's simply no way to appease this kind of creature. He'll always take too much, as he demonstrates when he eats her arm, followed by the rest of her body. This is essentially a cautionary tale, with the implication that the wife foolishly ignored her husband's wisdom, opening the door to her own death.

# BEAN SIDHE

## IRELAND

The bean sidhe, usually anglicized as "banshee" but with many spelling variations, is an Irish . . . fairy? Out of all the creatures in the book, her supernatural status is one of the most hotly debated. Scholars have suggested that she's the offspring of a fairy and a mortal, a changeling, an abducted human woman, a fallen angel, or the spirit of an unbaptized child. Or maybe she's a descendent of Tuatha Dé Danann, a ghost bent on revenge, a soul stuck in some kind of purgatory, or a woman who has become entirely consumed by grief. Pick your poison. Realistically, there's not going to be a tidy answer on this one, and luckily, for our purposes, we don't need one. She's a magical, supernatural creature who profoundly touches human lives, so she fits right under our fairy umbrella.

What the bean sidhe definitely is is a female spirit who haunts a specific family. When a family member is about to die, she wails to mark their death. This cry might only be heard by the relevant family, or it might be audible to anyone nearby. The quality of the scream varies, and it might sound like a fox or dog, an especially powerful human scream, or completely unearthly. Despite being hard on the ears, the bean sidhe is usually extremely beautiful, but just to mix it up, she occasionally appears as a very old woman. She usually has long, lustrous hair, which she brushes with a special comb. This has led to the development of stories about the danger of picking up lost combs. In these tales, someone finds a beautiful comb, picks it up, and then promptly has massive regrets when they're terrorized by screaming and wailing all through the night. The screaming only ends when the comb is put back where it was found. Sometimes, long tongs are used to return the comb through a window, and the tongs are destroyed in the process!

Folklorist Lady Wilde describes the bean sidhe thusly: "Sometimes the Banshee assumes the form of some sweet singing virgin of the family who died young, and has been given the mission by the invisible powers to become the harbinger of coming doom to her mortal kindred. Or she may be seen as a shrouded woman, crouched beneath the trees, lamenting with veiled face;

or flying past in the moonlights, crying bitterly: and the cry of this spirit is mournful before all other sounds on earth, and betokens certain death to some member of the family whenever it is heard in the silence of the night."

It's not entirely clear whether the bean sidhe actually causes the family death by choosing to scream or if her cry simply functions as an omen of a death that she otherwise has nothing to do with. Which one you believe shapes how sinister the bean sidhe is to you.

# BAKRU

## SURINAME AND GUYANA

Bakru look like small children but with quite the caveat. Only half of their bodies is flesh and blood. The other half is made of wood. Anna Claybourne writes that "they have large heads with big, black eyes, and always appear in pairs—one male and one female." Some stories say that you can enter into a demonlike deal with them (think *Faust*) and trade your soul to them for protection and wealth. Others say that bakru love to set fires and pelt unsuspecting humans with rocks. Fun fact: They mostly eat bananas and milk, which is kind of a refreshing change from all the cannibalism!

# DUPPY AND JUMBIES

## CARIBBEAN

Duppy and jumbies are especially tricky to pin down, as this can be a bit of a catchall term for malevolent spirits that bring ill fortune to those unlucky enough to cross their paths. Most of their activity happens at night. They may appear as small fairies that live in silk cotton trees, or kapok trees. These trees themselves are also said to be magical and to have the power to uproot themselves from the ground and walk around at night. It's considered very bad luck both to cut down such a tree or to plant one too close to your home. Alternatively, duppy and jumbies may be spirits of the dead with an affinity for human possession. In other stories, they're shapeshifters who may take on the guise of a cat, bull, or pig. There's a lot of variation in this fairy type, due to differences in cultural influences—we're talking Dutch, Chinese, South American, and more—in the places where duppy and jumbies appear, but they're virtually always associated with death and bad news.

# DYBBUK

## JEWISH

The dybbuk is a spirit from Jewish folklore that has roots in the Talmud, an approximately 1,500-year-old text central to Judaism. Part ghost, part demon, the dybbuk is a human spirit that, because of sins perpetrated during his lifetime, seeks to possess a living body. The only way to exorcize a dybbuk was to appeal to a rabbi, the only person who could successfully drive him away. Stories about these spirits were "especially prevalent in 16th–17th-century eastern Europe," and they've increased in popularity since "the Jewish scholar and folklorist S. Ansky contributed to worldwide interest in the Dybbuk when his Yiddish drama *Der Dybbuk* (c. 1916) was translated into several languages." A few recent horror movies and attention-grabbing hoaxes have contributed to the resurgence as well.

# PONATURI

## NEW ZEALAND

The ponaturi are part of Māori folklore, and they basically function as goblins of the sea. They're often depicted as red-haired and sharp-clawed. By day, they live in a land beneath the sea, and when night falls, they come ashore to sleep. We've got shades of vampire here, because it seems that the reason they must return to the sea before sunrise is that the sun is dangerous, even fatal, to them! Anna Claybourne writes that they "recite their magic spells aloud, beating out a rhythm with stolen human bones." They show up in various Māori legends and myths including tales of Tāwhaki, a kind of demigod. For instance, after the ponaturi kill or kidnap his parents, Tāwhaki tricks the creatures into thinking it's still night by blocking the light from entering the house they're inside. He then lets the sun pour in, killing the murderous ponaturi inside.

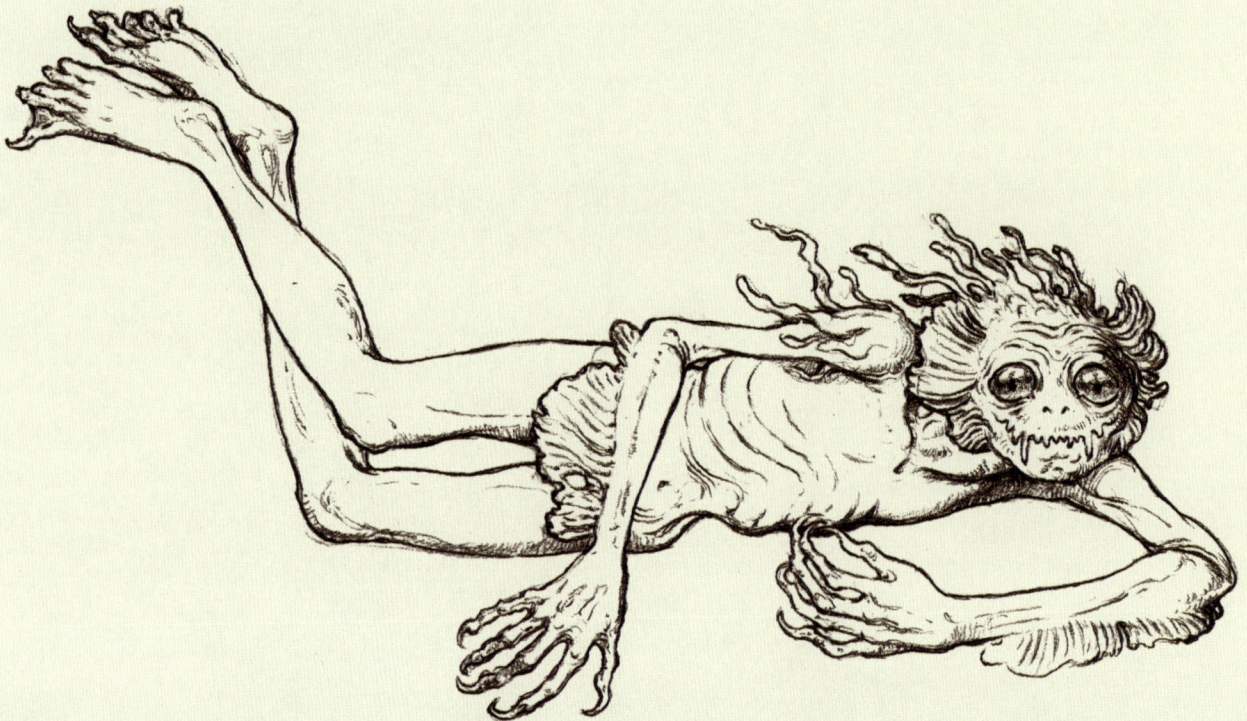

# KAKAMORA

## SOLOMON ISLANDS

Kakamora are a tiny, gnomelike tribe found in the folklore of the Solomon Islands. Standing at about six inches, they wear a head covering made of coconut. They're said to have super long hair and fingernails, and the latter are sharp and deadly. They make their home in limestone caves and prefer to come outside only when it's raining, which is incredibly adorable. However, when they come out of those caves and into the rain, it's often to snatch unwary travelers and lost children, which are their preferred snacks. Lore suggests that they're terrified of the color white and will flee back to their caves if they see it.

# DEEV

## IRAN

Deevs are monstrous supernatural creatures from Persian folklore. From there, they've mingled with Islamic cultures, spreading broadly and picking up local variations as they go. They exist alongside and have been known to occasionally overlap with other supernatural creatures of South and Central Asian beliefs, including jinn, peri, and shayatin. Peri are usually good, or at least amoral, but deevs . . . not so much. They're often depicted as massive, hairy ogres with horns and tusks. Sometimes, they have snakes for hair— and sometimes, they *are* snakes! In addition to being physically strong, many deevs can also wield magic, which they like to use to torment their victims with nightmares. Depending on the tale, they might eat a human or abduct them or just generally be incredibly contrary, always doing the opposite of what they're told. A noted deev pastime is capturing peris (which are often smaller and more delicate) in cages they hang in tall trees. Delightfully, other peris can bring their friends perfume to inhale as sustenance, which keeps them alive until they can escape!

# RÁKSHASA

## INDIA

Rákshasas are "malevolent magical being[s]," similar to demons or goblins, that appear in the *Ramayana*, *Mahabharata*, and *Kathasaritasagara*, as well as other sources of Hindu mythology. They have supernatural powers but live on earth, and they're known for disrupting sacrifices, eating people, and taking up residence in cremation grounds. During the daytime, their powers fade, and so they're active and making mischief at night. They can shapeshift at will, appearing as "as animals, as monsters, or in the case of the female demons, as beautiful women." The most powerful of the rákshasas is their ten-headed king, Rāvaṇa.

Not all rákshasas are equally or intrinsically evil; some are more akin to yakshas, or yakṣas (nature spirits), while others are similar to asuras, the traditional opponents of the gods. In fact, Rāvaṇa even has a virtuous brother who was also a rákshasa. The term, however, most often pairs with cemetery haunting, a diet of human flesh, and cow milk theft.

Rákshasa stories can get pretty graphic. Here's an excerpt from "Story of Aśokadatta and Vijayadatta" to give you a sense of just how sinister (and hungry) these creatures can be!

> The brave Vijayadatta . . . laughed and said in his confidence,
> "What can the wretched goblins and other evil ones do to me?
> Am I a weakling? So take me there without fear." When he said
> this so persistently, his father led him there, and the boy warming
> his body approached the pyre, which seemed to bear on itself the
> presiding deity of the Rákshasas in visible form, with the smoke
> of the flames for dishevelled hair, devouring the flesh of men. The
> boy at once encouraged his father and asked him what the round
> thing was that he saw inside the pyre. And his father standing
> at his side, answered him, "This, my son, is the skull of a man
> which is burning in the pyre." Then the boy in his recklessness
> struck the skull with a piece of wood lighted at the top, and clove

it. The brains spouted up from it and entered his mouth, like the initiation into the practices of the Rákshasas, bestowed upon him by the funeral flame. And by tasting them that boy became a Rákshasa, with hair standing on end, with sword that he had drawn from the flame, terrible with projecting tusks: so he seized the skull and drinking the brains from it, he licked it with tongue restlessly quivering like the flames of fire that clung to the bone. Then he flung aside the skull, and lifting his sword he attempted to slay his own father Govindasvámin. But at that moment a voice came out from the cemetery, "Kapálasphoṭa, thou god, thou oughtest not to slay thy father, come here." When the boy heard that, having obtained the title of Kapálasphoṭa and become a Rákshasa, he let his father alone, and disappeared.

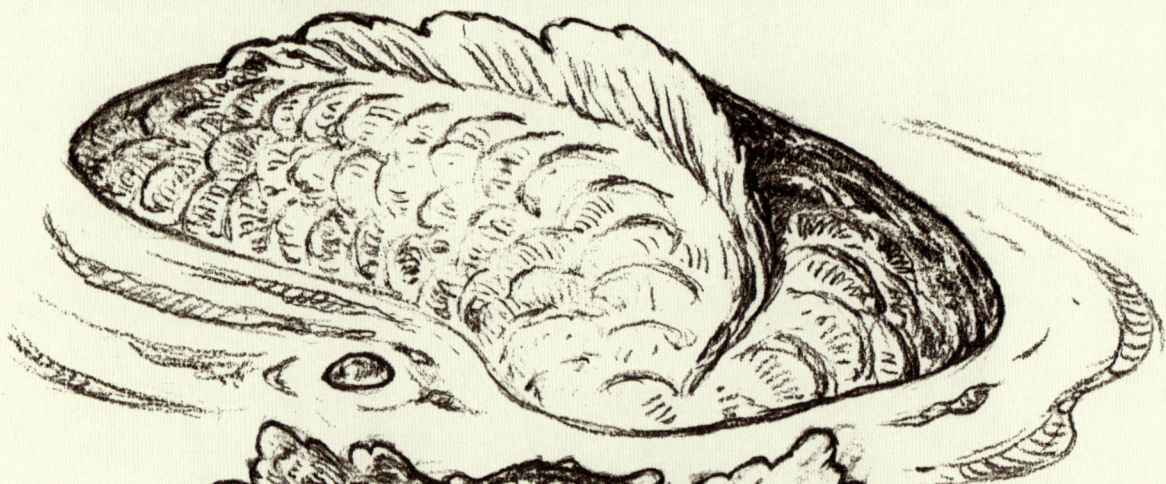

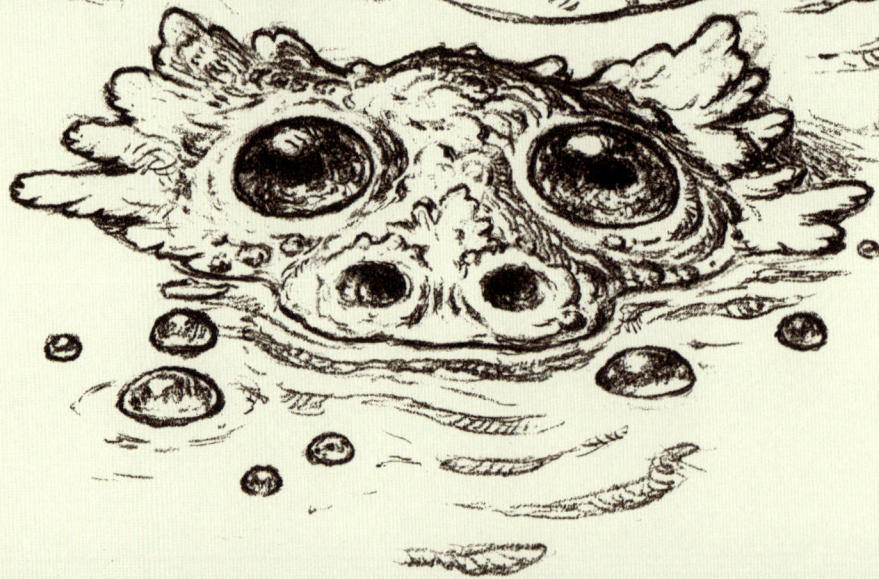

# BUNYIP

## AUSTRALIA

An aquatic, perhaps even amphibious creature from Australian Aboriginal folklore, the bunyip can be found in swamps, lagoons, and other wetlands. Depictions of this guy are . . . inconsistent. There are images and descriptions that range from humanlike to hippopotamus-adjacent. They can look like a manatee or a cat or a fish or a seal or even something completely alien. One account from 1847 describes the bunyip as a gigantic starfish! The bunyip does love to boom or roar, especially when in pursuit of devouring its favorite prey: human women and children. It's been speculated that the bunyip may have been inspired by rare seal sightings and bird cries.

# KAMIKIRI

## JAPAN

Kamikiri, or kamikiri-ma, translates as the haircutter or the haircutting demon, and it does what its name says it does: It cuts hair, suddenly and inexplicably, in contexts where no one should be receiving a haircut! This might sound funny, but imagine that somehow, between the office and walking in your front door, your long hair has been chopped off into a bob, and you have no idea how or when it happened. (Spoiler: It would feel creepy, upsetting, and violating!) The kamikiri is the entity blamed for this phenomenon.

Stories of this bizarre and inexplicable haircutting seem to have circulated in the Edo period as an urban legend and were recorded in collections like *Shokoku rijindan* (1743) and *Mimi bukuro* (1814). And these creatures do seem to be distinctly urban, with stories about them spreading through cities. There were tales of people walking home at night and realizing when they arrived home that their hair had been cut off at the point where it was tied. Presumably, their hair was lying in the street somewhere. The kamikiri didn't just go after women—they also loved cutting men's hair, too.

To us, this can seem nonsensical and harmless, especially since haircutting is hardly deadly and the kamikiri aren't murderous the way so many other fairies in this chapter are. But hair is culturally symbolic, and this is especially true in the relevant period in Japan and in Japanese culture in general.

Michael Dylan Foster, a folklorist specializing in Japanese culture, explains why the haircut blitzes of the kamikiri would feel so threatening:

> In Heian-period texts such as *The Tale of Genji*, long luxurious female hair projected beauty, sexuality, and wealth. In *Genji*, as well as later military tales such as *The Tale of the Heike*, both women and men cut off their hair on becoming Buddhist nuns or monks. The phrase "cut off one's hair" became a kind of shorthand for taking religious vows and renouncing the material world. At other times, too, such as the genpuku coming-of-age ceremony held to celebrate a boy's initiation into manhood, cutting off hair represented a symbolic change in status. Throughout the Edo period, hair also revealed a great deal about people: women's hairstyles could vary with age, marital status, social position, and employment. For men, the topknot (chonmage) transmitted information on status, profession, and lineage. All this is to say that the Kamikiri resonated meaningfully in Edo society: having your hair cut suddenly and without your knowledge would have been a violent physical and symbolic experience.

Perhaps because the kamikiri does his work unseen, descriptions of his physical appearance can be sparse. Still, in stories and illustrations, he can be fox-like, insect-adjacent, or even humanoid. He may have razor-like hands or teeth or simply carry scissors with which to stealthily snip his victims' hair.

# NIX

The nix is a truly spectacular case study of why fairy categorization is always an exercise in futility. It goes by a number of names, including but not limited to nixie, nixy, nix, näcken, nicor, nøkk, and nøkken across German and Scandinavian regions. We considered folding it in with kelpies because it's often regarded as another water horse, but also it's often described as half human and half fish. And as a generalized shapeshifter. And as a wyrm or a dragon. And as a Germanic melusine. And as a Germanic rusalka. Sometimes, nix are described as exclusively male . . . and sometimes as exclusively female. They can seduce and repel and eat humans and marry them and drown them—in no particular order. They're usually malevolent, but they also love music and art and dancing and can be bought off with gifts. They might appear as a strapping man, an old woman, or a fair maiden. We could have put this fairy almost anywhere in this book and made a case for it.

# ASWANG

Likewise, we must at least mention the aswangs of the Philippines and acknowledge up front that there's simply no way to pin them down accurately. "Aswang" is an umbrella term, and it has been used to refer to almost any kind of malevolent creature you can imagine. They are often shapeshifters with the ability to hold many forms, but they can be witches, ghouls, vampires, human-animal hybrids, and more, depending on the location and tradition the story comes from. They may suck blood, wield magic and curses, or eat corpses, but almost all of it is going to be bad news for the humans who cross their paths.

# KELPIE

## SCOTLAND, UK

The kelpie is a water horse from Scottish and Irish folklore, and it is *sinister*. Folklorist Katharine Briggs calls it "bloodthirsty" and "hungry for human life." Its true form is said to be a horse, but it can also take the shape of a man. Even when wearing a human shape, its true nature might be given away by the shells and weeds that tangle in its hair. In both shapes—and the occasional other animal forms it might take—it tends to be dark-haired or luminously bright, and it's strikingly beautiful and compelling. And its hair is, chillingly, always wet, no matter how long it has been out of its native water. That water is usually fresh water—kelpies are creatures of lakes and rivers, working as a kind of cautionary tale to keep people, especially children, from straying too close to the water's edge.

Kelpie stories do not end well for the humans they encounter. Kelpies will attempt to lure humans onto their backs, and if a human is foolish enough to mount a kelpie, they've signed their death warrant. Once astride a kelpie, there's no way to dismount—this will be the human's final ride. The kelpie will race back to their river or lake, where it will drown the human and then gobble them up.

For instance, Briggs shares a story from Glen Keltney (noting that very similar tales can be found all over the Highland lakes):

> One story commonly told was of seven little girls who were out walking on a Sunday, and saw a pretty little horse grazing near the lochside. One after another they got on its back, which gradually lengthened itself so that there was room for them all. A little boy who was with them noticed this, and refused to join them. The horse turned its head, and suddenly yelled out, "Come on, little scabby-head, get up too!" The boy ran for his life, and hid among the boulders where the thing could not get at him. When it saw this it turned aside and dashed into the loch, with the seven little girls on its back. And nothing of them but their entrails ever came to land.

Entrails. We told you: kelpies don't mess around.

Famed Scottish poet Robert Burns immortalized the kelpie in his poem "Address to the Devil" (1786), writing:

> When thowes dissolve the snawy hoord,
> An' float the jinglin icy-boord,
> Then water-kelpies haunt the foord
> By your direction,
> An' nighted trav'lers are allur'd
> To their destruction.

Kelpies don't always kill the humans they meet, though kelpie clemency is the exception rather than the rule. In some stories, they take human lovers, sometimes with a willing human and sometimes through assault or rape, and other stories tell the tale of the half-kelpie children who result from these encounters.

Kelpies are, of course, far from the only legendary water horse you'll find in fairylore. There's the Welsh ceffyl dŵr, the Manx capaill uisce, and, of course, the German nix (discussed in a sidebar on page 122), among others, and they all have their own distinctions.

# IFRIT

## ISLAMIC

ʿAfārīt are powerful, malevolent supernatural creatures found in Islamic folklore. They often have wings made of smoke, and they live underground or in ruins (#mood). They have complex family structures, are resistant to human weapons, and are susceptible to magic.

"Ifrit" is ultimately a pretty nebulous term, but the vibe is rebellion, strength, and wickedness. An ifrit *could* be good . . . but they're usually not, preferring to be ruthless and disruptive. They can be understood as demons, spirits of the dead, or creatures of the underworld.

ʿAfārīt do not seem to exist in pre-Islamic poetry, but they do appear once in the Qurʾān. They also feature widely in literature as well as folklore, including multiple tales collected in *One Thousand and One Nights*.

Nizami Ganjavi, a twelfth-century Muslim poet, wrote of the ifrit in his romantic epic *Haft Peykar*, or *Bahramnameh*, in the story of Māhān, an Egyptian wayfarer. As part of his adventures on a demon-infested desert, Māhān encounters a beautiful girl with the face of a Peri in an oasis. Disregarding the warnings of his host, Māhān embraces the girl . . . who abruptly turns into a terrifying ifrit! She's described thusly:

> from mouth to foot had her existence from the wrath of God.
> A buffalo with boars teeth such that none would think a dragon
>    could so (monstrous) be.
> A hunch-back,—God defend us (all)!—a hump like that of bow, a
>    bow that's drawn in
> Tūz,
> Her back a bow, her face was like a crab; her stinking odour
>    reached a thousand leagues.
> A nose (she had) like a brick-makers kiln; (she had) a mouth (too)
>    like a dyer's trough.
> Her lips apart like jaws of crocodile

The ifrit prepares to tear Māhān apart for his disobedience and lustful thoughts, but he's saved when a rooster crows at the returning dawn and everything demonic vanishes. (Roosters: saving men from being supernatural toast globally for thousands of years.)

# JINNI

## ARABIC

The jinn come from Arabic mythology, and they're a fairly catchall family of spirits "inhabiting the earth but unseen by humans, capable of assuming various forms and exercising extraordinary powers." They appear in the Qur'ān, and, like humans, they're capable of choosing good or evil, meaning they can achieve salvation or earn damnation. Historically, they were believed to inspire poets and prophets. They "are beings of smokeless flame by nature, in the same manner in which humans are said to be made of earth, and they cannot be seen by human beings." They've long been a staple of folklore and literature, and their inclusion in texts like *The Thousand and One Nights* introduced them to ever wider audiences. In folklore, "jinn are capable of assuming human or animal form and are said to dwell in all conceivable inanimate objects—stones, trees, ruins—and underneath the earth, in the air, and in fire. They possess the bodily needs of human beings and can even be killed, but they are free from all physical restraints." A few of the specific varieties of jinn include ghūl (ghouls) and ʿafārīt (evil baddies).

# TIKOLOSHE

## SOUTH AFRICA

Tales of the wicked water sprite, the tikoloshe, are common in Zulu, Sotho, and Xhosa legends. They're heavily associated with witchcraft, to the point that they're often cast as a witch's familiar. They're pretty tiny, standing at about knee height, but they're humanoid in shape and covered with hair or fur, giving them the general appearance of a baboon. They can move about invisibly, remaining unseen to the humans they encounter. And they also apparently possess exceptionally long, flaccid penises that are carried slung over their shoulder. This fits with Rachel King's remark that "the image or trope of the tikoloshe is a powerful one in Nguni and Sotho folklores, and often denotes improper sexual appetites, mischief upon and theft of cattle, and vengeance wrought by practitioners of magic." In general, they seem to be amorous in nature and likely to steal milk and otherwise mess with cattle. And their obsession with cattle has a deeper meaning, one that mirrors their propensity to steal sexual fluids for their own magical and medical uses. Because cattle are key to marriage—in fact, they make marriage possible through the bridewealth exchange—the tikoloshes are interfering with the foundations of social bonds and sanctioned reproduction.

Tikoloshes are actually said to be the source of a witch's power—by being a familiar, they allow a witch to work their magic. According to Monica Hunter Wilson, the tikoloshe familiar "is of opposite sex to that of the witch and is often spoken of as taking the form of a beautiful girl or a handsome man, very light in color, and the witch and familiar have sexual relations. Usually the familiar is acquired by inheritance. The basis of these beliefs is again dreams, sex dreams being frequently interpreted in terms of witchcraft." These familiars are culturally understood to be evil, and without redeeming qualities or the ability to be harnessed for good.

As you may have noticed from their physical description and interaction with witches, tikoloshes are pretty sexually charged. Anthropologist Isak Niehaus has a source that claims the tikoloshe's penis is elastic and that he can use it to poke into places to feel around and make sure it's safe. Some of his other informants claim that tikoloshes could be female, in which case they have huge breasts that fill a similar function as the male tikoloshe's penis. Additional Niehaus informants say that you can get a tikoloshe from a root, others say that you could change a domestic animal into a tikoloshe using animal fat, and still others say that the witch and the tikoloshe were actually the same, that the witch "smear[s] animal fat on their own bodies to transform themselves."

Niehaus believes that, though the tikoloshe can be used for many purposes from protecting a witch's home to stealing from neighbors, the "*tokolose* symbolizes illicit sexual desires," "unrestrained" desires, and that definitely tracks with the stories from his informants. He writes that "witches are believed to set off at night as the *tokolose* to commit evil deeds and to rape sexually desirable women and men in the neighbourhood. In this form they are invisible and possess exceptional strength and sexual prowess. One informant argued that witches were more inclined to act themselves in the form of the *tokolose* than to send it out by itself." Tikoloshes can also take on the appearance of their witch or even function as a kind of changeling. For example, a witch might sleep with someone and then, while her lover sleeps, she'll depart but leave behind her tikoloshe, which has changed shape to look like her. For instance, Niehaus "was told of a young man who slept with the daughter of a well-known witch, whilst making love to her he felt that she was ice cold and hairy. When he spoke to her, her voice responded from outside the room. The young man fled, thinking that he had made love to a *tokolose* which looked like his girlfriend." Despite this seeming usefulness, some stories say a tikoloshe can kill his witch, while others say there is "an essential unity" between them and that "if the familiar is killed the witch would also die."

Tikoloshes are sometimes associated with isindiyandiya, an herb that grows from a potato-like root. Isindiyandiya grows underwater and is said to contain some of the tikoloshe's power.

# KAPPA

## JAPAN

One of the most famous of Japanese yōkai, kappa are associated with water, and they're often found by rivers, ponds, and swamps. They're usually scaly, slimy, and green in color, and they have webbed feet and hands. Basically, they are suited for an aquatic environment. Most distinctively, they have a carapace or shell on their backs—like the shell of a turtle. They may have the overall appearance of a turtle, too, but they can also look like a frog or monkey. Though they're small, usually about the size of a child, kappa are superhumanly strong, which they use to their advantage when fighting, drowning, and generally making trouble. One of the kappa's most striking features is the concave indentation on the top of their heads. This bowl-like depression is filled with water—if the water on top of a kappa's head spills, he'll lose his incredible strength.

Kappa are highly mischievous and sometimes deadly. They're known to pull cattle, horses, and sometimes small children into the water to drown them.

Despite this, kappa are also playful and honest. They love sumo wrestling, and stories frequently feature them issuing wrestling challenges to people who walk by their rivers.

In a pinch, bow to a kappa, especially before a sumo match. He will bow back and spill the water from the top of his head!

Kappa are enthusiastic eaters, and not just of humans. They love melons, eggplants, and cucumbers. You might have noticed that your cucumber sushi roll is often called a kappa maki after kappa.

Folklorist Michael Dylan Foster explains that "numerous local rituals and festivals, particularly in agricultural communities that depend on water for irrigation, celebrate kappa as water deities (suijin). When treated appropriately, the local kappa will ensure ample water for irrigation; if neglected or treated with disdain, it will cause drought or flooding. The kappa, therefore, can be considered simultaneously a deity and a demon, depending on the perspective of the human beings with whom it is in contact." Foster also

clarifies that "kappa" is one word among more than one hundred local variations, including "kawappa," "kawako," "enko," "dangame," and others. Many
of these names refer to an animal the kappa may resemble, like a monkey or
otter, while others refer to the creature's behavior rather than appearance.

Arguably the oldest written incident of the kappa, or kappa-like creature,
that we know of can be found in the *Nihonshoki* (720 CE), in which a snakelike
creature kills travelers who venture too close to a river. Kappa really became a
yōkai staple during the Edo period, appearing in local legends, popular illustrated books, and even academic texts. Delightfully, the cultural resonance
of the kappa has taken a real turn in recent years. According to Foster, "This
slimy creature that once terrorized people and animals venturing near the
water has now become a symbol of unspoiled nature. You can find cutesified
kappa images posted near rivers, imploring people not to litter or spoil the
environment. In other words, a yōkai that used to represent the violence and
unpredictability of the natural world, and especially water, has now literally
become a poster child for the effort to stop the sacrifice of nature."

# DOMOVOI

## SLAVIC COUNTRIES

The domovoi is a Slavic house spirit that is sinister but usually not deadly. He likes to mess with people while they sleep, in a style that's very similar to the mara and other creatures said to cause sleep paralysis.

According to folklorist Natalie Kononenko, the domovoi is the "essence of the home" but also representative of the "inverse of human behavior." He's nocturnal and extremely active at night, and he prefers work that's traditionally coded as feminine. He might even help out those in the household who are especially industrious. He's often paired with and even said to be married to the domovikha, a female house spirit. Like the bean sidhe, he can herald the death of family members in the house he's attached to. But he's most famous for his interference with those who slumber under his roof.

Like other sleep paralysis tales, stories about the domovoi tend to be told in first person, and they're usually "memorates," which is a subcategory of legend that shares personal experiences. In other words, instead of saying that this happened to a friend's sister's boyfriend or to a woodcutter in Germany in 1723, it's something that happened to the narrator. Domovoi stories take place when the narrator is asleep or just about to doze off, almost always at night. The narrator might report seeing a dark, hairy shape by a door or the window, and they might hear footsteps as the creature approaches their bed. As the domovoi approaches, the narrator starts to feel pressure being applied to their body, usually starting low on the body with feet or ankles and steadily rising until they feel like their chest is being crushed. According to Kononenko, "Supposedly, the proper thing to do in this situation is to ask the house spirit whether he has come for good or for ill. He will either answer and disappear, or he will laugh and vanish. The type of laugh foretells good or ill fortune, with 'ha, ha, ha' meaning something good will come and 'hee, hee, hee' predicting misfortune. Narrators agree that, while misfortune predicted by the *domovoi* cannot be averted, being prepared for it makes things easier."

The domovoi, it appears, can be reasoned with, or at least dealt with, if you know how. We don't love the idea of coexisting with a sinister, strangling house spirit, but at least you can be prepared.

# How Thomas Connolly Met the Banshee

By J. Todhunter

## IRELAND

W. B. Yeats included J. Todhunter's "How Thomas Connolly Met the Banshee" in his *Fairy and Folk Tales of the Irish Peasantry*, and it's a perfect example of how bean sidhe stories tend to go! We particularly love the description of the fairy's eyes: "blue as two forget-me-nots, an' as cowld as the moon in a bog-hole of a frosty night, an' a dead-an'-live look in them that sent a cowld shiver through the marra o' me bones."

Aw, the banshee, sir? Well, sir, as I was striving to tell ye I was going home from work one day, from Mr. Cassidy's that I tould ye of, in the dusk o' the evening. I had more nor a mile—aye, it was nearer two mile—to thrack to, where I was lodgin' with a dacent widdy woman I knew, Biddy Maguire be name, so as to be near me work.

It was the first week in November, an' a lonesome road I had to travel, an' dark enough, wid threes above it; an' about half-ways there was a bit of a brudge I had to cross, over one o' them little sthrames that runs into the Doddher. I walked on in the middle iv the road, for there was no toe-path at that time, Misther Harry, nor for many a long day afther that; but, as I was sayin', I walked along till I come nigh upon the brudge, where the road was a bit open, an' there, right enough, I seen the hog's back o' the ould-fashioned brudge that used to be there till it was pulled down, an' a white mist steamin' up out o' the wather all around it.

Well, now, Misther Harry, often as I'd passed by the place before, that night it seemed sthrange to me, an' like a place ye might see in a dhrame; an' as I come up to it I began to feel a cowld wind blowin' through the hollow o' me heart. "Musha Thomas," sez I to meself, "is it yerself that's in it?" sez I; "or, if it is, what's the matter wid ye at all, at all?" sez I; so I put a bould face on it, an' I made a shruggle to set one leg afore the other, ontil I came to the rise o' the brudge. And there, God be good to us! in a cantle o' the wall I seen an ould woman, as I thought, sittin' on her hunkers, all crouched together, an' her head bowed down, seemin'ly in the greatest affliction.

Well, sir, I pitied the ould craythur, an thought I wasn't worth a thraneen, for the mortial fright I was in, I up an' sez to her, "That's a cowld lodgin' for ye, ma'am." Well, the sorra ha'porth she sez to that, nor tuk no more notice o' me than if I hadn't let a word out o' me, but kep' rockin' herself to an' fro, as if her heart was breakin'; so I sez to her again, "Eh, ma'am, is there anythin' the matther wid ye?" An' I made for to touch her on the shouldher, on'y somethin' stopt me, for as I looked closer at her I saw she was no more an ould woman nor she was an ould cat. The first thing I tuk notice to, Misther Harry, was her hair, that was sthreelin' down over her showldhers, an' a good yard on the ground on aich side of her. O, be the hoky farmer, but that was the hair! The likes of it I never seen on mortial woman, young or ould, before nor sense. It grew as sthrong out of her as out of e'er a young slip of a girl ye could see; but the colour of it was a misthery to describe. The first squint I got of it I thought it was silvery grey, like an ould crone's; but when I got up beside her I saw, be the glance o' the sky, it was a soart iv an Iscariot colour, an' a shine out of it like floss silk. It ran over her showldhers and the two shapely arms she was lanin' her head on, for all the world like Mary Magdalen's in a picther; and then I persaved that the grey cloak and the green gownd undhernaith it was made of no earthly matarial I ever laid eyes on. Now, I needn't tell ye, sir, that I seen all this in the twinkle of a bed-post—long as I take to make the narration of it. So I made a step back from her, an' "The Lord be betune us an' harm!" sez I, out loud, an' wid that I blessed meself. Well, Misther Harry, the word wasn't out o' me mouth afore she turned her face on me. Aw, Misther Harry, but 'twas that was the awfullest apparation ever I seen, the face of her as she looked up at me! God forgive me for sayin' it, but 'twas more like the face of the "Axy Homo" beyand in Marlboro Sthreet Chapel nor like any face I could mintion— as pale as a corpse, an' a most o' freckles on it, like the freckles on a turkey's egg; an' the two eyes sewn in wid thread, from the terrible power o' crying the' had to do; an' such a pair iv eyes as the' wor, Misther Harry, as blue as two forget-me-nots, an' as cowld as the moon in a bog-hole of a frosty night, an' a dead-an'-live look in them that sent a cowld shiver through the marra o' me bones. Be the mortial! ye could ha' rung a tay cupful o' cowld paspiration out o' the hair o' me head that minute, so ye could. Well, I thought the life 'ud lave me intirely when she riz up from her hunkers, till, bedad! she looked mostly as tall as Nelson's Pillar; an' wid the two eyes gazin' back at me, an' her two arms stretched out before hor, an' a keine out of her that riz the hair o' me scalp till it was as stiff as the hog's bristles in a new hearth broom, away she glides—glides round the angle o' the brudge, an' down with her into the sthrame that ran undhernaith it. 'Twas then I began to suspect what she was. "Wisha, Thomas!" says I to meself, sez I; an' I made a great struggle to get me two legs into a throt, in spite o' the spavin o' fright the pair o' them wor in; an' how I brought meself home that same night

BUNWORTH BANSHEE FROM *FAIRY LEGENDS AND TRADITIONS OF THE SOUTH OF IRELAND* BY THOMAS CROFTON CROKER, PUBLISHED 1834

the Lord in heaven only knows, for I never could tell; but I must ha' tumbled agin the door, and shot in head foremost into the middle o' the flure, where I lay in a dead swoon for mostly an hour; and the first I knew was Mrs. Maguire stannin' over me with a jorum o' punch she was pourin' down me throath (throat), to bring back the life into me, an' me head in a pool of cowld wather she dashed over me in her first fright. "Arrah, Mister Connolly," shashee, "what ails ye?" shashee, "to put the scare on a lone woman like that?" shashee. "Am I in this world or the next?" sez I. "Musha! where else would ye be on'y here in my kitchen?" shashee. "O, glory be to God!" sez I, "but I thought I was in Purgathory at the laste, not to mintion an uglier place," sez I, "only it's too cowld I find meself, an' not too hot," sez I. "Faix, an' maybe ye wor more nor half-ways there, on'y for me, shashee; "but

what's come to you at all, at all? Is it your fetch ye seen, Mister Connolly?" "Aw, naboclish!" sez I. "Never mind what I seen," sez I. So be degrees I began to come to a little; an' that's the way I met the banshee, Misther Harry!

"But how did you know it really was the banshee after all, Thomas?"

"Begor, sir, I knew the apparation of her well enough; but 'twas confirmed by a sarcumstance that occurred the same time. There was a Misther O'Nales was come on a visit, ye must know, to a place in the neighbourhood—one o' the ould O'Nales iv the county Tyrone, a rale ould Irish family—an' the banshee was heard keening round the house that same night, be more then one that was in it; an' sure enough, Misther Harry, he was found dead in his bed the next mornin'. So if it wasn't the banshee I seen that time, I'd like to know what else it could a' been."

135

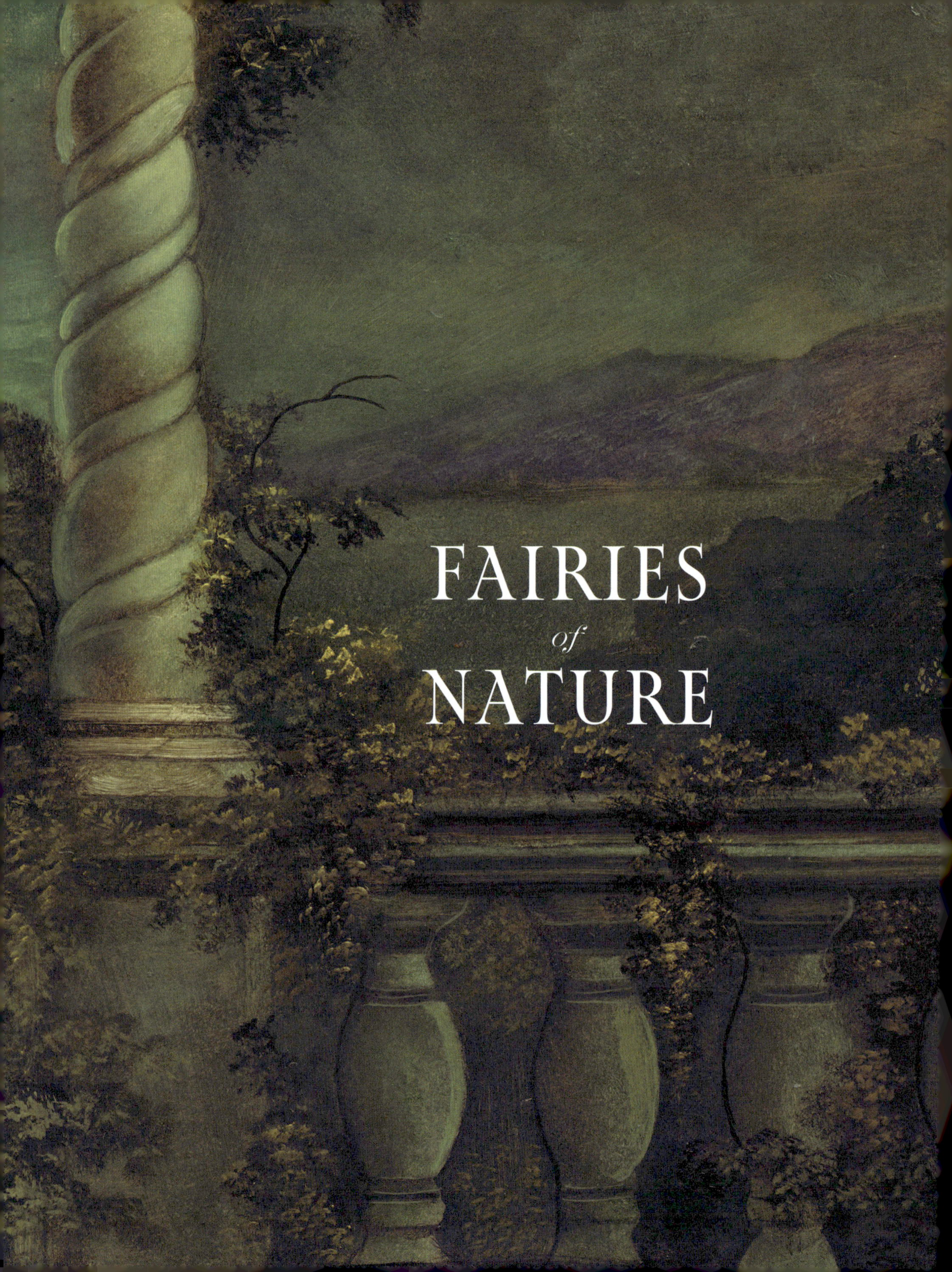

# CHAPTER 4

# FAIRIES *of* NATURE

While fairies of the home, fairies of seduction, and fairies of terror are likely to seek out mortal company, for both kind and nefarious purposes, there are plenty of fairies who dwell at a remove, often in the depths of the wild. Though we mentioned in our introduction that fairies are not always connected to nature, the fairies in this chapter are often tied closely to specific rivers, trees, or mountains. Some of them even serve as guardians of their homes, a folkloric connection that has inspired environmental activists today to link these fairies to causes from forest preservation to river clean-ups. Frankly, we get it, as disturbing the environments around these creatures is usually ill-advised. As the protectors and spirits of natural spaces, they are very, very likely to lash out when their habitat is threatened.

Even today, the power of nature fairies can be felt. For example, in 1999, a fairy tree caused a lot of trouble for a planned upgrade to the M18 motorway in Latoon, County Clare, Ireland!

# THE CAILLEACH BHEUR

## SCOTLAND, UK

In Scotland, the Cailleach Bheur is, basically, the personification of winter. She's frequently even depicted as an old woman with a blue face, fighting off the coming of spring with her staff, a device she uses to magically freeze the ground. She is said to be the daughter of the winter sun and the guardian of wild animals. Every year, she's reborn so that she can bring back the snow and ice. When spring does finally defeat her, as it inevitably must, she throws her staff down under a holly tree and transforms into a gray stone. Afterward, green grass refuses to grow there. She's often seen herding deer through the wintry landscape, though many animals—wild goats and wolves among them—also hold a special place in her heart.

This fae creature—or at least one very similar in appearance—is a fixture throughout the British Isles, though she goes by many similar, but distinct names. She is known as the Cally Berry in Ulster, Ireland; Black Annis in Leicestershire, England; Gentle Annie in the Lowlands; and the Old Woman of the Mountains in Wales. Because she's so widely known, Katharine Briggs suspects she may be a remnant of a lost mythical figure similar to Artemis, the Greek goddess of wild animals. She may have even been an inspiration for stories like "The Marriage of Sir Gawain" and Chaucer's loathly lady in "The Wife of Bath's Tale" from *The Canterbury Tales* because, in some tales, she doesn't turn to stone at the end of winter but rather into a beautiful maid.

# CURUPIRA

## BRAZIL

The curupira is a goblin-like fairy with orange hair evocative of fire. He lives in and protects the Amazon rainforest of Brazil. His name actually means something like "covered in blisters," which, you know, isn't super appealing. His feet face backward, which makes him easy to spot as long as you know what you're looking for. He dresses all in green, often rides a collared peccary (a hoglike creature), and enjoys taking care of animals, especially mothers and their children. He's not a big fan of human hunters, but he'll tolerate them . . . unless you take more than you need or just hunt for fun—in which case, you're in trouble. As Anna Claybourne notes, the curupira will punish you by making trails of his backward footprints, which are deliberately designed to get you lost in the rainforest forever. He is also said to be able to make illusions, animal sounds, smoke, and strange whistles to escalate your confusion, so we really don't recommend messing with this guy. Adrian Burton writes that the curupira was once said to have a garden in the Amazon as well, a strange place where you'll find nothing growing but huitillo trees. In a location as diverse as the rainforest, this can seem supernaturally bizarre. Scientists have now figured out that a specific kind of ant is responsible for this type of strangely homogeneous place, but, as Burton points out, the curupira is the protector of such creatures, so you might as well still consider it his garden and leave well enough alone. Fun fact: In 1970, the Brazilian state of São Paulo designated this guy a state symbol and official guardian of forests and animals!

# PERI

## IRAN

Peris are "delicate, winged creatures, glowing with shimmering, multicolored light" from Persian folklore. They're usually depicted as female, with the ability to perform magic and acts of sorcery. Unlike the deevs, who love to antagonize and war with them, peri are usually kind and helpful to humans they encounter. They don't eat food, at least not in the way you'd expect. Instead, they survive "merely on the aroma of exquisite perfume." Interestingly, their wings are often depicted as more birdlike than the butterfly or mothlike wings we've become accustomed to associating with fairies in the West.

Peris can be incredibly alluring to humans, but these unions are usually ill-fated. These stories often feature broken taboos, with a human man refusing to follow his peri wife's enigmatic requests. When he breaks the rules, the peri must leave him.

# VELI

## FIJI

The veli creatures of Fiji are very small, usually male, gnomelike spirits. They live in the forest, typically in places like hollowed-out trees, and you can hear them singing or sighing in the woods. These guys even have actual wings sometimes. They're also notable for their glowing eyes and the fact that they're extremely hairy. Colonial official Adolph Brewster speculated in 1922 that their "large fuzzy mops of hair" were "miniatures of what [the people of Fiji's hair] were like until they were cropped in deference to the sanitary requirements of the Wesleyan missionaries," a little subversive "screw you" to colonialism that we support. Matt Tomlinson's article in *The Journal of Polynesian Society* describes them as "decidedly contrary," a description we feel is delightfully appropriate. Overall, they are fairly well regarded, even to the point that they are considered "relations," but you don't want to get on their bad side. They are powerful in both magic and physical strength, and some people say that they experience everything in the opposite way that humans do. For example, when something is hot to a human, the veli would experience it as cold!

# ANAR PARI

## INDIA

The anar pari is, we are delighted to tell you, a tiny fairy from Indian folklore who lives in pomegranates. According to the tale, a young son of a king wants a perfect bride. His mother tells him that he'd better marry the "Anar Pari" then (sometimes the "queen of the Anar Pari" or the "queen of the Anardes"), "who is the fairest of all fairies." The prince responds, "Alright, bet," and sets off on a very difficult undertaking. Eventually, however, he's able to escape the dragons who guard the fairy in her pomegranate home, and she agrees to marry him. This story has a lot of shocking, even deadly, twists and turns, and we enjoyed it so much that we made it our example story for this chapter. That said, we do have a special note for this one.

The story of the anar pari comes to us via two collection of Indian stories, the first called *Simla Village Tales or, Folktales from the Himalayas* published by Alice Elizabeth Dracott in 1906, and the second called *Folk Tales of Sind and Gujarat*, published in 1925 by C. A. Kincaid. In both retellings, there is some pretty strong evidence of Westernizing throughout, presumably to make it more familiar and palatable to their mostly British audiences. We still wanted to include these fairies (let's face it, pomegranate fairies are awesome) but this context is important to acknowledge.

# PÚCA

## IRELAND

The Irish púca, whose name simply translates as "spirit" or "ghost" and can also be written as puca, wwca (in Wales), pooka, phouka, phooka, and pouk (in England), is what W. B. Yeats calls "essentially an animal spirit." These fairies are shapeshifters who can transform into all kinds of animals, but most often horses, goats, dogs, cats, bulls, eagles, and rabbits. They may also take on a human form, but you can usually spot them because they'll retain distinctive animal features like a tail.

Púcaí can be helpful or malicious, but usually they're just mischievous in character. They like to play tricks and might try to entice humans to ride on their backs while they're in horse form. Usually this would involve scaring them silly by taking them on a terrifying ride, but they don't generally try to drown or otherwise kill their victims and will usually deposit them back where they found them. This sets them apart from, say, the members of the Wild Hunt or the distinctly murderous kelpies. It's all in good fun for púcaí (thought their victims might disagree). If you want to try to go on one of these wild púca rides, you might try wearing spurs, as this can sometimes tame them a bit!

Yeats relates a story told by Douglas Hyde that he believes is likely the story of a púca doing some mischief: Hyde said, "Out of a certain hill in Leinster, there used to emerge as far as his middle, a plump, sleek, terrible steed, and speak in human voice to each person about November-day, and he was accustomed to give intelligent and proper answers to such as consulted him concerning all that would befall them until the November of next year. And the people used to leave gifts and presents at the hill until the coming of Patrick and the holy clergy." We're inclined to agree—that definitely sounds like púca-like behavior!

Now, you might be wondering, is the púca at all linked to Shakespeare's famous shapeshifting fairy, Puck from *A Midsummer Night's Dream*? Take a look at this passage from act 3, scene 1, where Puck describes himself:

I'll follow you, I'll lead you about a round,
Through bog, through bush, through brake, through brier,
Sometime a horse I'll be, sometime a hound
A hog, a headless bear sometime a fire;
And neigh, and bark, and grunt, and roar, and burn,
Like horse, house, hog, bear, fire, at every turn.

That sounds almost exactly like the púcaí we've been describing, no? We didn't mention it at the beginning, but the word "puck" has indeed also been used to describe a similar creature throughout the British Isles. In fact, scholar Wirt Sikes argues for a Welsh influence in particular, noting that "there is a Welsh tradition to the effect that Shakespeare received his knowledge of the Cambrian fairies from his friend Richard Price, son of Sir John Price, of the priory of Brecon. It is even claimed that Cwm Pwca, or Puck Valley, a part of the romantic glen of the Clydach, in Breconshire, is the original scene of the 'Midsummer Night's Dream'" So is Puck a púca? Our guess is yes!

# ATLIARUSEK

## CANADA AND GREENLAND

The atliarusek are small, gnomelike creatures that can be found in Canada and Greenland, according to Inuit legends. They are said to live underground, especially in rocks near the sea, and they even paddle tiny kayaks around. They don't like to be seen by humans—if they see you first, they'll vanish—but they can be helpful, especially to hunters.

In one story, "The Girl Who Married an Atliarusek" collected by Hinrich (Henry) Rink and published in 1875, an atliarusek marries a human girl in secret, staying hidden because he isn't sure her parents will approve of him. He brings them all kinds of food, and the wife's father keeps saying that he should stay and live with them, but he remains elusive. Eventually, he tells them he must go away with his own kind on a hunting expedition, and the wife's father insists that he and his daughter come with them. They sail along with the fairies until "the head-man of the atliaruseks" tells them to keep close to the fairy-boat's wake. Then, suddenly, the fairy "boat sink[s] beneath the surface, and totally disappear[s]"! This is understandably pretty upsetting for the father and the daughter, but they're right behind it, so when they hit the same spot, "their boat dive[s] down in the same manner, without any damage to the crew." They quickly catch up to the fairy-boats and "continu[e] their course beneath the waves of the sea. Having safely passed the inhabited places, they once more r[i]se to the surface, and continu[e] their voyage without further peril." They eventually get to an area with bountiful hunting, and become very well off, and the wife's father ends the story showing off his amazing son-in-law to the men who wanted to marry his daughter that he rejected for her husband, proudly claiming that his new fairy son was far better than any of them.

Now, boats that move underwater are all well and good, but here's our favorite piece of lore about these guys: According to Anna Claybourne, some tales say that the Atliarusek actually hunt tiny polar bears!

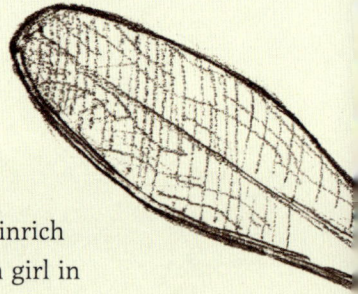

# KORPOKKUR

## JAPAN

The korpokkur are fairies said to live in the northernmost part of Japan and are part of the folklore of the Ainu people, an Indigenous group. "korpokkur" basically translates to "the people who live under the butterbur plant," and it is said that they use the leaves from this plant to make their roofs (hence their name). Supposedly they were there long before the Ainu people themselves, but when they did meet, they were friends at first. The korpokkur are very small, but skilled fishermen, so the human Ainu and the korpokkur traded with each other, with the one caveat being that the korpokkur did not like to be seen and only brought their trades at night. The story goes that, one day, a man decided he wanted to see one, so he grabbed a korpokkur woman by the arm when she was outside and brought her into the light. She was so mad that all the korpokkur went into hiding and, according to Anna Claybourne, "have never been seen since."

Fun fact: In the fourteenth installment of the Japanese *Final Fantasy* video game series, there is a korpokkur character. They depict him as a small, round, green fellow with a butterbur leaf growing out of his head.

# LESHY

The leshy, also sometimes known as the leshen or lyeshy, is a forest creature known throughout ancient Slavic folklore. According to W. R. S. Ralston's 1872 book, *The Songs of the Russian People*, the leshy can change his shape and stature whenever he likes, making himself taller than trees or even smaller than a blade of grass. He can assume a humanlike shape, too, but he's usually pretty easy to spot. He never has any eyebrows or eyelashes, and *Britannica* adds that he might have a more than usually pointed head and be missing his right ear as well. Ralston notes that, in his true shape, he has horns on his forehead, goat feet, long claws, and is covered with long, often green, hair. He's generally considered a mischievous fairy, but he's sometimes even downright malicious. He's often found sucking the milk from cows, laughing and running through the woods, and fighting with others of his kind. You really don't want to be around when that happens though, because their weapons are huge trees and rocks, which they like to hurl at each other.

Don't ever stop to rest in a cave that might belong to a leshy either—if he finds you there, he might transform into a whirlwind in an attempt at terrifying you into leaving (he's also sometimes associated with wind, storms, etc.). If that doesn't work, you can bet you'll be very lost the next day. He can alter landmarks, transform himself to look like trees that weren't there before, and do all kinds of things designed to make sure you never make it home.

He is considered the protector of the forest and all the animals who live there, especially bears and wolves. Like the curupira, he'll allow some hunting, but only if you make an offering to him first. Like rusalki, he's been known to tickle people to death, but if you find a baby leshy in the forest and take care of him, you may be rewarded. You can summon a leshy by cutting down young birch trees, placing them in a circle (tops facing inward), standing in the middle, and shouting "Grandfather!" . . . but we're not really sure that's advisable.

Fun fact: Most of the time, the leshy is considered a forest spirit, but some Slavic places also have leshy of the cornfields, who grow and diminish alongside the corn harvest!

# WILL O' THE WISP

## UK

Most of the time, will o' the wisps are depicted as ghostly lights seen at night, most often in marshes, swamps, and bogs—in other words, places with access to water. They are infamous for luring the unwary astray on unfamiliar ground and getting travelers lost in misty, marshy landscapes, sometimes leading to their permanent disappearance or death. Imagine this scenario: A man is out hunting, and he gets a little lost. He sees what he thinks is a light in front of him and he thinks, "Oh, thank God—a light! Someone else is out here! Maybe it's even a house!" He moves toward it, which seems like the logical move. However, that isn't a light; it is a will o' the wisp, and the man is actually just going deeper into the marsh or swamp and becoming more and more lost.

Will o' the wisp personalities range from mischievous to malicious. They might simply lead travelers around in circles or into a ditch, but the more sinister of them could lead travelers right off a cliff or into water deep enough to drown them or, as in our example, just get these people so lost in the marshes that they never make it home.

Strength, size, and color varies widely. They may be faint or extremely bright, a flickering candle-flame size to a roaring torch, and any color from blue, to green, to white, to orange. In some tales, a will o' the wisp may be a human spirit that has been cursed or barred from the afterlife and so must wander the nights carrying a light. Like many similar tragic fairies, they are often assumed to be the remains of young girls. Other possibilities from the folklore include liars, cheats, or the spirits of unbaptized children.

There's also the problem of their name. There are many, many names for will o' the wisps. Some identified by Katharine Briggs include "fool fire," from the Latin *Ignis Fatuus*, Bill with the wisp, Hobbledy's lantern, Jack-a-lantern, Jenny-with-the-lantern, Jenny-burnt-tail, and many more. While the will o' the wisp is usually considered to be its own distinct entity, it's also possible to think of it as an umbrella term for a wide range of fairies who look and behave the same way: providing a bright light in the darkness and showing a tendency to lead unwary travelers astray. Sometimes will o' the wisps also blur with other folkloric fairies, like the Welsh death-candle. W. Y. Evans-Wentz writes that an anonymous Welsh woman told him (via her nephew, who was translating for her) that "the death-candle appears like a patch of bright light; and no matter how dark the room or place is, everything in it is as clear as day. The candle is not a flame, but a luminous mass, lightish blue in color, which dances as though borne by invisible agency, and sometimes it rolls over and over. If you go up to the light it is nothing, for it is a spirit. Near here a light as big as a pot was seen, and rays shot out from it in all directions. The man you saw here in the house to-day, one night as he was going along the road near Nevern, saw the death-light of old Dr. Harris, and says it was lightish green." This story supports the idea that will o' the wisps are (or at least are connected to) the spirits of the dead. In New Orleans, there are also tales from Cajun folklore of the fifolet, small fairies who appear as flickering blue lights in the swamps. Fascinatingly, stories of these fairies were first recorded by Alexis de Tocqueville in his famous book *Democracy in America*.

This fairy is particularly interesting because it so clearly straddles the line between supernatural creature and natural phenomenon. Since fairylore is part of legend, which is rooted in place, there's always some connection to the context and landscape from which the folklore emerges, but this is extra explicit in the case of the Will o' the Wisp. Basically, Will o' the Wisps are always seen around water because, the theory goes, they are actually bioluminescent swamp gasses caused by animals and plants going through the process of organic decay.

Morgan Daimler writes that "The Will o' the Wisp is an interesting thing to study, possibly a ghost or a fairy from one view and a swamp phenomena by another, one that may be explained by scientific means but whose folklore persists. There is a debate even today about whether the Will o' the Wisp is supernatural or a natural occurrence." As folklorists, we'd honestly argue that this debate largely misses the point; legends exist to help explain the unexplainable and to address cultural fears and anxieties, and that's exactly what will o' the wisps do.

We would be remiss if we didn't mention the fact that there are often fairy animals throughout the world as well—animals that are, as Katharine Briggs puts it, "magical in themselves, with special powers and an independent way of life, fairies in animal form that is, and the fairy domestic animals, different from human cattle and often of a superior breed, but appurtenances of the fairies." It seems that fairies can have pets and livestock of their own!

In the UK, animals belonging to fairies "are often described as red and white"—that's how you know not to mess with them. Briggs goes on to note that fairy animals can also be "made of rushes or stems of ragwort transformed at a word," that "sometimes they have special powers and wisdom," and that "sometimes they are beautiful miniature creatures, which can rise through the air as lightly as a flight of starlings." She worryingly adds too that some may be "enchanted men and women" so . . . perhaps keep that top of mind!

Fairies do also seem to be fond of certain kinds of animals like horses and cows. Briggs writes that "of the wild birds, swans, ravens, swallows, robins and wrens have the greatest magical association," but we'd argue that fairies have a definite soft spot for cats, too. If you've ever seen a cat intensely staring at nothing and then *chasing* that nothing, you likely agree. Briggs notes that, in Ireland at least, "cats are regarded almost as fairies in their own right," and quotes from W. W. Gill's *A Second Manx Scrapbook* (1932) that there is a "Manx belief that the cat was the only member of the family whose presence was tolerated by the fairies when they came into the kitchen at night." In the Scottish Highlands, there was even a

FAIRY ANIMALS

creature known as the Cait Sith, the cat fairy, who was large and black with a white spot on his front. You could appease him by offering him milk! In Norse folklore, Norwegian Forest Cats are known as "fairy cats" and may indeed have been the inspiration for the enormous cats said to pull the goddess Freyja's chariot.

In Hindu mythology, there is Garuda, a great bird who serves as the mount of the god Vishnu and strikes us as very fairylike. According to *Britannica*, he "is described in one text as emerald in color, with the beak of a kite, roundish eyes, golden wings, and four arms and with a breast, knees, and legs like those of a kite. He is also [sometimes] depicted anthropomorphically, with wings and hawk-like features."

Last, we'll mention the black dog of England, sometimes known as a grim or a church grim, a capelthwaite, padfoot, or shag. This is a large, black spectral dog with fiery eyes, who some say guards churches from evil spirits and/or roams the English countryside. Seeing him may prove to be an ominous event. The sight is said to foretell a death. One of the most famous of these fairy dogs is the Black Dog of Peel Castle. According to Briggs, it would be "death to touch" him, but he was also "known to give friendly warnings of disasters at sea. On one occasion it held back the skipper of a fishing boat so that he did not put to sea, and so escaped wreck in a sudden storm that sprang up." Interestingly, this tradition may have crossed the Atlantic. In the Maryland and West Virginia areas of the US, there's also a black dog–like cryptid figure called the snarly yow!

# YAKSHA

## INDIA

Yakshas are nature spirits of India who serve as the protectors and guardians of the forests. They also guard any treasures that may be found there. They're usually able to do all kinds of magic and to shapeshift, which obviously makes spotting one extra tricky. They're usually pretty sexually aggressive so, you know, be careful out there.

In personality they range from kind to mischievous to downright murderous. In one story from the Jātaka tales, an Indian collection of stories mostly about the previous births of Gautama Buddha, a merchant and his fellow travelers meet with a group of yakshas disguised as gentlemen wearing soaking wet clothes. The yaksha tell the men that they were drenched in a pouring rain and that all of the bodies of water along their route are overflowing with water, so the men decide to get rid of all the water they're carrying. With all the abundant water everywhere, why mess with carrying it? Well, of course the forest they enter is dry as a bone, they all die of thirst, and the yakshas feast on their bodies.

These creatures have a complex mythology, including a leader named Kubera, who is said to rule a mysterious Himalayan kingdom called Alaka. He is commonly associated with prosperity and is considered a protector figure. This mythology may go all the way back to the early Indigenous people of India, and specific yakshas even sometimes serve as tutelary deities—gods and goddesses of specific cities or districts. Yaksha worship was very common for a period, and in the realm of sculpture, yakshas are said to be "among the earliest of deities to be depicted, apparently preceding images of the bodhisattvas and of Brahmanical deities, whose representation they influenced."

# NUNO SA PUNSO

## PHILIPPINES

The nuno sa punso, whose name means "grandpa of the mound," live in the forests of the Philippines. They are small fairies with long beards, and they typically make their dwellings in ant's nests or mushroom mounds. As Anna Claybourne notes, they really hate to be disturbed, so if you step on one of their mounds—even by accident—they tend to curse you with "swollen feet, aches and pains, or even a hairy back!" Some say they can even cause you to vomit blood, form lesions, and experience other, even more dangerous afflictions as well. Modern medicine usually doesn't have much of an impact on a nuno sa punso curse, but profound apologies and offerings may work, as might going to a faith healer instead, according to an informant speaking with folklorist Napoleon Martinez. In fact, it's said that if you even just *see* one of these mounds, you should immediately excuse yourself and affirm that you mean no disrespect, just in case. Stories of the nuno sa punso are often used to scare children into coming home before it gets dark. These mounds are harder to see in the dark, obviously, and avoiding a curse is a good incentive to get home on time.

# NAGA/NAGINI

## INDIA

Nagas and naginis are "semi-divine being[s] with a human face and the hood and tail of a cobra; dwellers in the under-world" or netherworld. Basically, they're half human and half snake. They appear across multiple Asian religious traditions including Hinduism, Buddhism, and Jainism, and they feature in the *Mahābhārata* as well as many local folk traditions. These creatures are often able to take a human, or partially human, form. They're strong and beautiful, and while, like any fairy creature, they can be dangerous to humans, they're often helpful, too. They feature heavily in art and literature where they're depicted in many ways: entirely human in shape but with snakes placed on their heads or necks, as fully serpentine, or as half human and half serpent. A female naga is called a nagi, or a nagini, and their descendants are known as nagavanshi and nair.

Nagaraja is the title given to the king of the nagas, and the nagas and naginis live deep underground in a kingdom called Naga-loka, or Patala-loka. This kingdom is resplendent with fabulous palaces and decorated with precious gems. Legend says that the god Brahma relocated them to this realm "when they became too populous on earth and commanded them to bite only the truly evil or those destined to die prematurely. They are also associated with waters—rivers, lakes, seas, and wells—and are guardians of treasure."

Additionally, nagas are often understood to be guardians of doorways and are even considered dragons in Southeastern Asian Buddhist folklore.

# AZIZA

## BENIN

The aziza are tiny forest fairies who live in the kapok trees and anthills of Western Africa, particularly what is now the area of Benin. According to Anna Claybourne, they are thought to be "the souls of the trees," and have been depicted with butterfly wings (a pretty cool attribute, considering how few fairies actually have butterfly wings, despite what British Victorians might tell you; that said, there does seem to only be one source for the butterfly wings, so maybe take them with a grain of salt). In a personal communication, anthropologist Timothy R. Landry told us that, more often, they're "deformed, hairy, and indeed—fairy-like." It is also said that, long ago, they gave a lot of practical advice to the first humans of the area, showing them things like "how to use plants as medicines, and how to make fire," as Claybourne continues. Unfortunately, humans got a little greedy, and "the shy Aziza retreated deeper into the jungle, which is why they are so hard to find today." However, according to Sarah Politz, a scholar of African music, the Aziza are also said to be "the source of all divine creativity, including musicians' ability to improvise and compose," so they still exert some influence in the world of humanity (even if they don't come out to play too often anymore!) Landry adds that we might consider aziza as "the force of inspiration. So, if someone is an incredible artist, dancer, or singer, folks will say they have a strong azizà. For example, the famous Beninoise singer Angelique Kidjo is said to have a strong azizà. Some have even said to me that she must be an azizà herself!"

All this taken together suggests that Aziza are forest spirits with a special affinity for trees and earth. Anthills are associated with fertility but also prophecy and sacred knowledge from West Africa into Central Africa. Silk cottonwood trees are also associated with knowledge due to their large size and intricate branch and root structures. Therefore, it's useful to think of aziza as part of the knowledge economy, especially of the wild. If you're lucky enough to see one (likely well outside a town) and approach it respectfully and convince it to talk to you, it will probably tell you something very worthwhile.

# The Anar Pari, or Pomegranate Fairy

*Retold by Alice Elizabeth Dracott*

## INDIA

The concept of fairies who live in pomegranates was simply too delightful to resist, so we had to choose their story for the "Fairies of Nature" chapter. Be forewarned, it packs quite a lot in, from fakirs to parrot transformations to dragons, but it also has the perfect mix of enchantment and danger for a good fairy legend. As we mentioned in the "Anar Pari" entry, Alice Elizabeth Dracott was an Englishwoman living in India in the early 1900s; thus we acknowledge the role that colonialism played in her collection of these stories. That said, we do also want to recognize that, in the preface of the collection, Dracott took pains to note that the translations she included are as "literal" as possible, and that "all the tales were taken down in pencil, just as they were told, and as nearly as possible in the words of the narrators, who were village women belonging to the agricultural class of Hindus in the Simla district."

Once upon a time there was a King who had seven sons, all of whom were married but the youngest.

One day the Queen-mother spoke to her youngest son, and said: "Why are you not married? Do not the maidens of my Court please thee? Perhaps you want what you cannot get, and that is perfection, unless, indeed, you go and seek and marry the Anar Pari, who is the fairest of all fairies, and whose charms are traditional."

The Prince then and there registered a vow that he would not marry at all unless he found this pearl of great price, and forthwith started on his quest for her.

He put on his armour and five weapons of defense, mounted his favourite steed, and set forth.

He had proceeded a good distance when night fell, and he found himself in a forest near a small hut. Entering it, he found it was occupied by a holy Fakir.

The Fakir said: "My son, why have you come here? Where are you going? And are you not afraid of the wild animals which infest this forest?"

The Prince replied: "Holy Father, I am going on a long journey to try and find the Pomegranate Fairy, so that I may wed her."

"You are going a long way indeed," replied the Fakir; "but if you listen to what I tell you, your journey will not be in vain."

Next morning he called the young man, and told him that he was going to enchant him and turn him into a parrot, so that he might fly to the island on which the fairy was imprisoned, and guarded day and night by seven hundred dreadful dragons. He also told him that on the island he would find a pomegranate tree with three pomegranates on it, of which he was to pluck and bring away the middle one, for in it dwelt the fairy he was so anxious to find.

"But mind you," said the Fakir, "once you have plucked the pomegranate, you are not to wait an instant, or even turn to look back when the dragons come after you, for, if you once look back, all your efforts will be in vain, and you will be killed."

Then the young Prince was turned into a parrot and immediately flew off.

He flew and flew and flew, till he had crossed seven seas; and in the midst of the seventh sea, he at last spied an island in which was a most lovely garden, where grew an exquisite pomegranate tree, and on it three pomegranates, the centre one most beautiful to behold.

He plucked the fruit, and flew as fast as he could, but alas, the dragon who guarded the tree saw him, and called to the other dragons, who, with wild yells and terrifying noises, flew after him.

The young Prince in his flight unfortunately looked back to see where they were, and was immediately burnt to a cinder, and fell to the ground with the golden pomegranate which he had worked so hard to obtain.

The dragons came up and took away the fruit, but left the burnt body of the bird upon the ground.

The Fakir waited long for the return of the parrot, but as it did not come, he set out himself to find it. He was able to cross in safety by making his body invisible, and when he came to the island, the first thing he saw was the burnt body of the parrot lying in the garden.

So he took it up, breathed once more the breath of life into it, and let it go, saying: "Try once more, my son, but remember that I said: 'Look not back,' but fly to my hut for safety."

Thus saying, he disappeared; and the parrot, watching its chance, very silently approached the tree a second time, stole the fruit, and flew as fast as he could.

The dragons pursued, but he reached the hut in safety; and the old Fakir did not lose a moment, but turned him into a small fly, and then secreted the pomegranate on his person, and sat down.

Almost immediately the dragons also arrived, and said: "Where is the green parrot who stole the fruit?"

"Look and see," said the old Fakir. "I know not what you want; no green parrot is here, nor do I know where the pomegranate is that he took away."

Then he went on quietly counting his beads while the dragons searched everywhere; but at last, wearied out and finding nothing, they went away, feeling very angry at the loss of their fairy.

As soon as they had gone, the Fakir caused the Prince to resume his original form, and, handing him the pomegranate, said: "Go back to your Palace; and when you have got there,

break the pomegranate, and out of it will step the most beautiful woman you have ever seen; take her to be your wife, and may luck go with you."

The young Prince then mounted his steed, and thanked the old Fakir for all his assistance.

As he neared his father's Palace he came to a well in a garden, and having tied his horse to a tree, he went and rested beside the well, and looked at the pomegranate.

"I think I will break it now, and see if a fairy comes out, for if I wait to do so in my father's house before all his courtiers, suppose no fairy appeared, I should be ashamed to death."

So saying, he broke it, and immediately a most lovely woman appeared, bright and dazzling as the sun itself. As soon as he beheld her, he was so entranced that he fell into a swoon. Then the fairy lifted his head very gently, and placing it on her knee, allowed him to sleep on.

While he slept a young woman of low caste came to draw water. Seeing the beautiful fairy, she enquired of her if the sleeping man was the King's youngest son, and if she was the Anar Pari whom he had gone to seek.

Hearing that this was so, she was filled with envy, and planned in her mind how she might take the life of the fairy. So she went up to her, and said: "O fairy, you are most beautiful, but I would be beautiful too if I had on your clothes: come, let us exchange our dresses (or sarees), and see how you look in my clothes."

The fairy did as she wished, and the young woman said: "Look how beautiful I am; let us go to the well and behold our reflections in the water to see which is the most beautiful."

The fairy bent forward to see herself, and, as she did so, the young woman pushed her so that she fell into the well and sank into the water.

Having done this, the wicked young woman woke up the Prince, saying: "Come, let us go to the King's Palace."

The Prince looked doubtfully at her, but, being still half asleep, and seeing that she wore the same dress as Anar Pari had on, he assented, believing his passing doubt to be unreasonable.

His arrival at the Palace was made an occasion for great rejoicings, and all were glad that he was at last happily married.

The new Princess would never allow him to leave her, for she feared that he might return to the well; but one day, unknown to her, he found his way there, and looking in, saw floating upon the water a most exquisite lotus lily of pure white, the most perfect flower he had ever seen.

He asked his servants to hook it out for him; but each time they tried to do so, the flower disappeared beneath the water. At last he tried himself to get it, and succeeded easily, for the lily floated towards the hook that he let down.

The Prince took the flower home and looked after it with the greatest care; but when his wife heard where it had come from, she went at night and, tearing it into several pieces, flung it out of the window.

As the broken fragments of the lotus touched the earth, they turned into a bed of mint which grew luxuriantly.

Some of this mint was earned into the King's kitchen, to be used for seasoning dishes; but as the cook began to fry it, a voice was heard from the frying pan, saying: "Here am I, the real Princess, being fried to death, while the wicked woman who threw me into the well has taken my place."

The cook when he heard this was afraid, and threw the mint into the garden again. As soon as it touched the ground it became a lovely creeper, which grew and grew until it gradually approached the bed-chamber of the Prince.

The false Princess when she saw it at once remembered how she had thrown the fragments of the lotus lily into the garden, and, fearing lest this might be an offshoot from it, she ordered her gardener to uproot the creeper and cut it down at once.

The gardener did so, but as he was removing it, the one and only fruit on the tree fell to the ground and rolled under a jessamine bush, where it remained in security.

The gardener's daughter, who came every morning to gather flowers from this bush to weave into garlands, accidentally noticed the fruit lying beneath it, picked it up, and carried it home.

As she entered the gardener's little hut, the fruit fell to the ground and broke open, and out of it stepped the lovely Anar Pari.

The good people of the house were filled with wonder and admiration to see so peerless a being in their humble cottage. They gave her shelter and fed her, the gardener's daughter loving her as a sister, and the gardener as a father.

One day, as the gardener's daughter sat weaving her garlands of jessamine for the King's Court, the fairy said: "Please allow me to make one too; and when it is ready, take it and put it on the neck of the youngest Prince."

So she made it; and when two garlands were completed they were taken to the Prince and Princess. The Princess noticed that the Prince's garland was made in wonderful fashion, and enquired who had made it. They told her that a very lovely woman living in the gardener's hut had made it, and, suspecting at once that this was Anar Pari come to life again, she thought of some plan by which she could destroy her.

The next day she feigned great illness and a very severe headache, which she declared nothing would cure but the placing of a heart of a young and beautiful girl on her forehead. She therefore begged for the heart of the girl who lived in the gardener's hut, and orders were given for her execution.

The gardener and his daughter wept most bitterly, and the executioners were feign to spare the life of so lovely a woman; yet they were obliged to fulfil their orders, so they led the girl to the place of execution.

Before they killed her she begged that her limbs might be scattered to the four winds, and her two eyes thrown upwards into space.

The executioners did as she desired, and her heart was sent to the wicked Princess.

As soon as Anar Pari's eyes were thrown into the air, they became a pair of love-birds and flew into the forest.

Many days after, the Prince went to hunt in the forest, and was resting himself under the trees when he heard two love-birds talking in the branches, and one was telling the other the story of her life. How she was once Anar Pari, a beautiful fairy, and how a wicked woman had enticed her away from the side of the Prince while he slept, and thrown her down a well, and how the woman was now reigning in her stead as Princess at the Palace.

The young Prince was amazed to hear all this, and looking up, cried: "I have at last found you. Come down and be my Fairy Princess once again."

Then two laughing, loving eyes appeared, and presently they were set in the form of a woman, and the Prince once again beheld the world-renowned form of Anar Pari.

They went together to the Palace, and there the Prince ordered the false Princess to be brought out, and told everybody present the story of her wickedness.

The sentence passed upon her was that she was to be buried alive near the well; this was done, and to this day nobody dare go near it. Then the Prince married the fairy, and they lived happily ever afterwards; but the old gardener and his daughter were not forgotten, and very often the beautiful Princess sat with her friends, and the two girls weaved garlands together, and spoke lovingly of the time when Anar Pari had dwelt in the old hut in the garden.

CHAPTER 5

# FAIRY NEIGHBORS

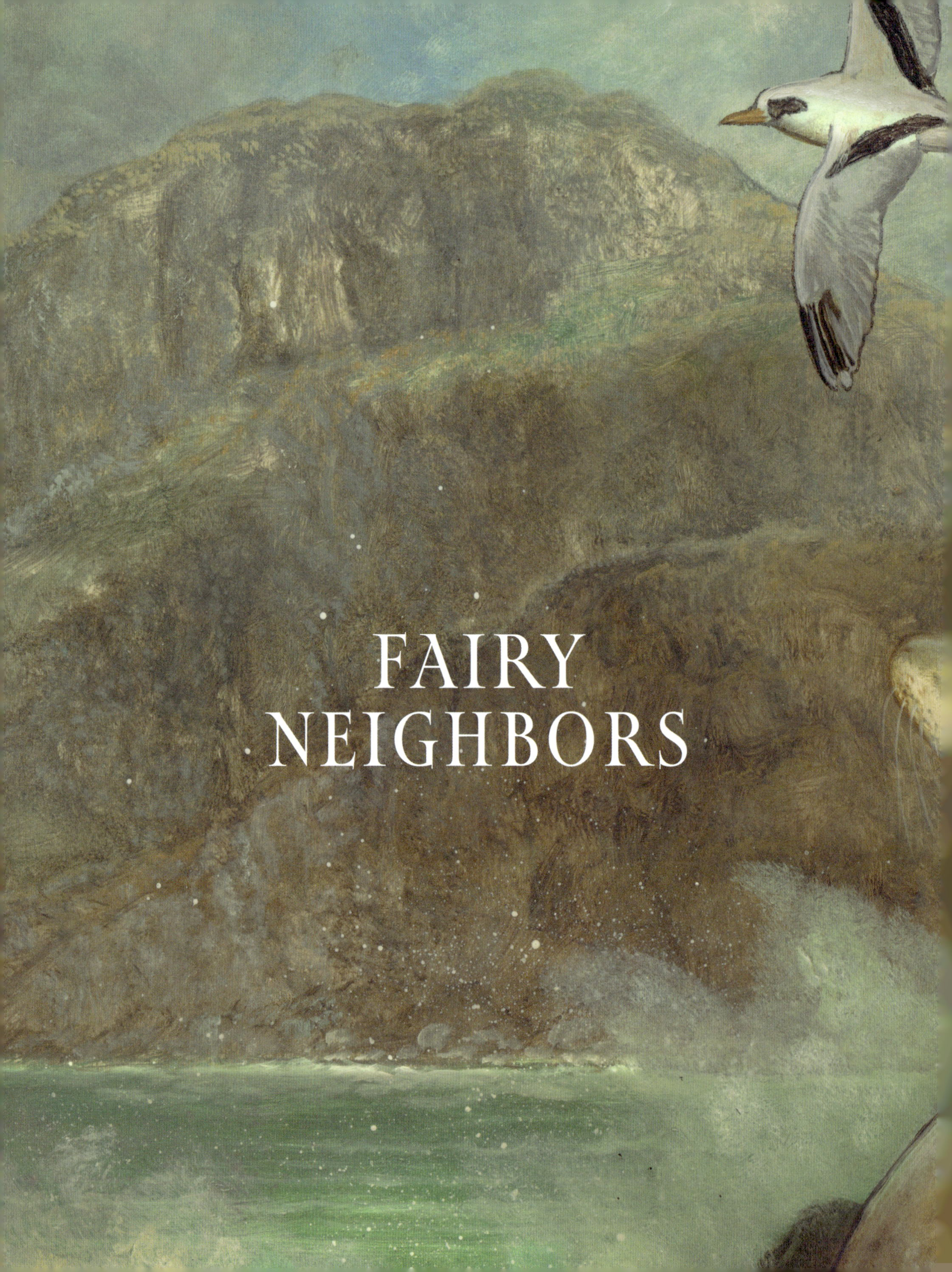

Katharine Briggs divides the British and Irish fairies associated closely with humanity into two types—"the ancestral fairy who is attached to a family, and who most commonly bewails coming tragedy or occasionally gives advice or even luck-bringing gifts, and the Brownie or hobgoblin who performs tasks, and attaches itself sometimes to a family and sometimes to a place. The last kind is much commoner and more widespread. There is some overlapping between them, of course, as there is in all folk tradition, but the main distinction is clear." In this chapter, however, we have a broader conception of what it means to be a "fairy of humanity," or "fairy neighbor," as we've titled it. It may mean fairies who have close, personal ties with humans or fairies who take care of humans in some way (or need humans to take care of them). Or perhaps it's fairies that do things for humans, or fairies who behave in particularly human ways. Or they may simply be the fairies who live among us . . . perhaps just next door.

# SHEYD

## JEWISH

Shedim, also sometimes called the mazikeen, the shideem, or the shehireem, appear in the Tanakh (the canonical collection of Jewish scripture) and Jewish folklore more broadly. They're most often referred to as spirits or demons, but to call a sheyd a "demon" really flattens the nuances of the term. They just don't line up with our modern conception of demons or the Christian understanding of evil demons in general. Shedim are not inherently evil. Instead, they're perceived as simply foreign or as not God, as *other* than God. They're often, but not always, violent. Indeed, they can be read as neutral, morally ambivalent, and even occasionally helpful. Folklorist Dan Ben-Amos suggests that "the term shedim may derive from the Akkadic sedu, a good spirit, representing a reversal of value attribution to an antagonistic religious system."

In addition to Jewish folklore, they also appear in the Christian Bible, where the word is usually translated as "devils." For example, Psalm 106:37 is translated as "Yea, they sacrificed their sons and their daughters unto devils" in the King James Version or "false gods" in some other translations. Marc Carlson writes in "Notes on a Demonic Pantheon" that shedim "possess the feet and claws of a rooster," though they are often described as having a human form. Legend says that if you sprinkle ash on the ground, it will reveal the shape of a shedim's footprints.

Multiple stories circulate about how the shedim came to be. One legend suggests that shedim are the descendants of serpents, connecting them to the story of the Garden of Eden. Others suggest that they are the children of Lilith, Adam's first wife, who refused his authority and became a demon herself. Another maintains that God began to create them on the sixth day but did not complete them when he stopped to rest on the seventh day. This means that shedim do not have true physical bodies, granting them the ability to shapeshift and take on whatever form fits their purpose.

Apparently, they enjoy jam. If you need to get on a sheyd's good side, offering them jam might be a good start. And like many supernatural creatures, they do not like salt, which can be employed as a barrier or deterrent.

# MENEHUNE

## HAWAII, USA

Menehune are small, humanoid creatures of Hawaiian tradition, and they're said to live in deep forests and valleys, far from human habitation.

Menehune are known for their incredible, even supernatural, craftsmanship, construction, and stonework. Legend says they built beautiful and sturdy temples, ponds, homes, boats, and roads, including many very old constructions that stand to this day. One of the ancient structures attributed to the menehune is a fishpond on Kauai.

Menehune are most active in their construction and craftsmanship at night. There are competing theories as to why this is the case. Some tales say it's because the menehune are lowly servants who are required to toil at night, while others suggest they prefer to work at night because they're wary of humans and want to avoid them. Still others insist it's because they're ancestral spirits who are just most active then by nature. Regardless, they don't like it when people mess with them while they're trying to work.

As Kim Martins points out, as far as we know, the menehune did not appear in stories recorded from the early European contact period, so it's very difficult to guess how old these stories are or where they came from. It's possible that stories of the menehune were a part of oral folklore, and that this knowledge was lost due to the cultural erosion of colonization.

What we can confirm is that menehune became especially popular in the 1860s when non-Hawaiian scholars and authors edited and published increasingly fantastical tales about mysterious entities with supernatural abilities. We're ultimately left with more questions than answers. Are the menehune a product of the Western imagination? Do they reflect knowledge of the first wave of Polynesian settlers? Are they a response to the escalating fascination with the nineteenth-century fairy tale, popularized by figures like Wilhelm and Jacob Grimm, Hans Christian Andersen, Peter Christen Asbjørnsen, and Jørgen Engebretsen Moe? Or were they part of a precolonial oral tradition? We simply don't know. However it began, the menehune are now a part of actively circulating Hawaiian folklore and culture.

# SELKIE

## UK

Selkies are shapeshifters who transform from human to seal and back again at will by donning or removing their sealskin coat. Their stories proliferate in Ireland and parts of the UK, but legends with similar themes and shapeshifters appear all over the world. There are male and female selkies, but most oral legends are about female selkies and mortal men. The basic story goes something like this: A man sees a selkie woman on the beach and falls in love or lust with her. To bind her to him, he steals her sealskin so that she can't go back to the sea or even leave him without leaving part of herself, and her ability to transform, behind. She begs him to return it, but he refuses. The man brings the selkie home with him and marries her, and eventually they have children. After many years, one of her children finds her sealskin and brings it to her, asking her what it is. She reclaims her skin and flees back to the sea, leaving her human family behind her.

Selkie stories return again and again to themes of love, loss, domestication, and wildness, and they're almost always very sad. Folklorist Katharine Briggs calls selkies "the gentlest of all" the fairies and notes that in stories they're "reluctant to avenge even the greatest injuries." And it's true that selkies don't tend to lash out against their human captors. But their stories offer us a way to talk about being trapped, about love and loss, and being forced to appear as something you're not. As Laura Marjorie Miller puts it, "The selkie story calls out to us for justice in territories of personal and natural concerns, in both cases about power." Selkies, or seal maidens, are among the most common fairy brides in British folklore, but as we said, there are tales of a seal husband marrying a mortal bride, too. The ballad "The Great Silkie of Sule Skerry" is such a tale. In this story, after the seal husband goes back to the water with their half-selkie child, the woman's second (human) husband winds up killing them both at sea, a fate he predicted.

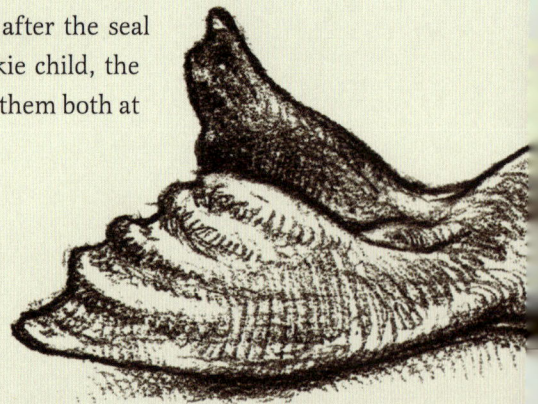

# HULDUFÓLK

## ICELAND

The huldufólk, or "hidden people," of Iceland live in rocks and crags. They live up to their name: You can see them only if you have a special ability or if they choose to show themselves to you. This is not exclusive to huldufólk (other places have similar beliefs attached to their fairies), but this does seem to be a key part of Iceland's fairylore.

In many ways, huldufólk are similar to humans in behavior and appearance, but they live in a kind of parallel world. The primary differences between humans and huldufólk seem to be that huldufólk are longer-lived and that female hulder have a hollowed-out back like a tree and sometimes a cow tail. Depending on the take, these female hulder can be portrayed as seduction fairies, too. Terry Gunnell writes that in huldufólk legends, especially the versions recorded in the eighteenth and nineteenth centuries, these fairies function as "near mirror-images of those humans who told stories about them—except they were beautiful, powerful, alluring, and free from care, while the Icelanders were often starving and struggling for existence. The huldufólk seem in many ways to represent the Icelander's dreams of a more perfect and happy existence."

According to Anna Claybourne, "Some people put small shelters for the Huldufólk in their gardens, or candles in their windows to light the way on New Year's Eve, when the Huldufólk are said to move home." This suggests to us that these fairies can be both human-sized *and* small.

# JOGAH

The jogah are small fairies that are part of the folklore of the six nations of the Iroquois Confederacy. Descriptions usually range from about knee-height to four feet, but they're consistently smaller than humans in stature.

They live within rocks and underground, and in some of the stories, their rocks can open up. When you go in, you'll find yourself in a whole fairy world! Like many fairies, they're visible only to some people, usually children, elders, and spiritual leaders. John Witthoft and Wendell S. Hadlock note that they're likely to go about in pairs—twins, a male and a female—and that they sometimes have no elbow joints! It's said at certain times you can hear them drumming in the forest.

They're usually friendly to Iroquois, especially if offerings like tobacco have been made, but they can also be tricksters. Anna Claybourne relays a legend of some jogah who help a small girl who's being ignored and neglected by her guardians, her aunt and uncle. The jogah give her food and then, delightfully and vengefully, send wolves to eat the feast her aunt and uncle are preparing—a feast that these guardians have determined to not share with their niece at all. She stays with the jogah for a while, but eventually they tell her she has to go back home, assuring her that everything will be okay because the aunt and uncle have "learned their lesson." This does seem to be true, as they're thrilled to see her and treat her like their own daughter from that day forward.

# LEPRECHAUN

## IRELAND

We feel confident that before picking up this book, you already knew of the Irish leprechaun, who has catapulted to fame far beyond the shores of his home. There is, however, a lot more to leprechauns than wearing green and being in possession of a pot of gold. According to scholar Diarmuid Ó Giolláin, the leprechaun is "a diminutive supernatural being of Irish folklore who is a shoemaker and possessor of great riches, for which is often pursued, and who through his characteristic cleverness and trickery usually gets the better of interfering mortals." He considers leprechauns to be "the artisans ('the tailors, brogue-makers, smiths, and coach-builders etc.') of the Irish fairies; they are usually seen in the evening in lonely spots during fine weather, 'are acquainted with all the hidden treasures of the earth' and escape their captors by distracting their gaze." Many accounts point to him as a shoemaker in particular, and he makes and repairs them for both mortals and fairies.

It was likely James Stephens's book, *The Crock of Gold* (1912), that popularized leprechauns on a global scale. Stephens's leprechauns are green-clad cobblers with pots of gold, but not all leprechauns match this description. They are, however, reliably small in stature. Ó Giolláin notes that, in many accounts, "he seems to observers to be old and wizened [. . . and] several accounts give him an ungainly, grotesque, aspect: he is a very small person with a big head and big feet, he is bandy-legged (this is a feature noted more than once) with big black eyes and long hairs." Other traits mentioned include "a very long nose," "pale," "hair [. . .] the color of skin," and teeth described as "bright." Perhaps most surprising: "Red is by far the [leprechaun's] favorite color, being mentioned in nearly three times as many accounts as its closest rival, green, which in turn is almost five times as common as black." They also seem to favor wearing some kind of faux suit-like outfit, a pointed hat, and large metal buckles on their shoes. They love tobacco, whistling, singing, and music, which they enjoy playing themselves, usually on a fiddle.

Leprechauns are usually solitary, living alone instead of in communities, and you're most likely to see one at times of high liminality, like early morning or sundown. They're also extremely wily, able to escape from captures under seemingly impossible circumstances—it's this characteristic that forms the centerpieces of many leprechaun legends. This uncanniness is aided by their occasional ability to shapeshift or go invisible.

As for the leprechaun's crock of gold, it actually is a pretty common feature in folklore, though Ó Giolláin adds that other things like "a pot of silver, a pot of money, a jug of gold, and a barrel of gold" are also mentioned. However, the end of the rainbow is usually not where it's stashed in the folk tradition. The idea of them having "purses" is also common, especially ones that endlessly resupply with money when you open them.

So are leprechauns bad or good? Honestly a bit of both. They're usually friendly enough unless you do something that would warrant revenge (like stealing from them, which, you know, fair).

In China, there's a beloved legend called "Dong Yong and the Seventh Fairy," or "The Fairy Couple," and Tian Xian Pei is the fairy heroine of the tale. The legend is known throughout China but also further afield, including Japan.

The plot goes something like this: The Jade Emperor, a godlike ruler, has seven fairy daughters, and they travel to the mortal world. The youngest of the daughters, Tian Xian Pei, is looking for her lost weaving tools and her magical coat of feathers, which grants her the ability to fly. Some versions specify that her coat was stolen by a mortal cowherd called Dong Yong, under advice from his bull who happens to actually be a fairy in disguise. Tian Xian Pei falls in love with Dong Yong, but he is impoverished and has sold himself into service to pay for the expenses of his father's funeral. The fairy maiden and her sisters work together to weave enough cloth to pay off his debts, but the Jade Emperor disapproves of the marriage and makes his daughter come home. But once a year, on the seventh night of the seventh month, the Jade Emperor allows Tian Xian Pei to fly across the Milky Way to visit Dong Yong.

According to scholar Wilt L. Idema, this legend has a fairly complicated history, but it can be traced all the way back to the second century CE and, even today, remains very popular. In fact, when discussing the legend in a paper, scholar David Holm writes that the story "is so well-known in China that it hardly bears repeating," and adds that there have been a variety of later additions to the tale as well, including one in which Dong Yong and Tian Xian Pei's son goes on a search for his lost mother. It has been made into numerous films, television shows, and other performances in China and beyond.

# TIAN XIAN PEI

# KONDERONG

## GAMBIA AND SENEGAL

Konderongs come from the Wolof culture in Western Africa, and they appear as small (two-foot-tall), gnomelike creatures who walk on backward-facing feet. Their beards are straight, white, and so long that the konderongs use them as clothes, draping and wrapping themselves in garments made from the flowing hair, linking them to water. Konderongs are tricksters at heart, and they're much more likely to toy with humans than to help them. According to Anna Claybourne, they're fond of pranks, which can range from the relatively benign, like using magic to prevent a human from putting down a heavy burden they're carrying, to the purely malevolent, like blinding people who cross their path or kidnapping children.

However, the folklore offers a silver lining to the troublesome konderongs: They possess an extremely valuable and magically potent treasure, a calabash, or water pot. If you can steal their calabash, its power can grant your wishes—not just one or three, but, legend says, *all of them*!

An important note: Anthropologist Misty L. Bastian strongly suspects that stories of the konderong are deeply inflected with cultural memories of the slave trade and European contact. Between the smooth hair, kidnapping, and a magical pot, there are a lot of clues to suggest this. Bastian really brought this home when she told us: "If you please the strange creature, it grants you wishes and wealth. If you don't, well, there's blindness and kidnapping in your future."

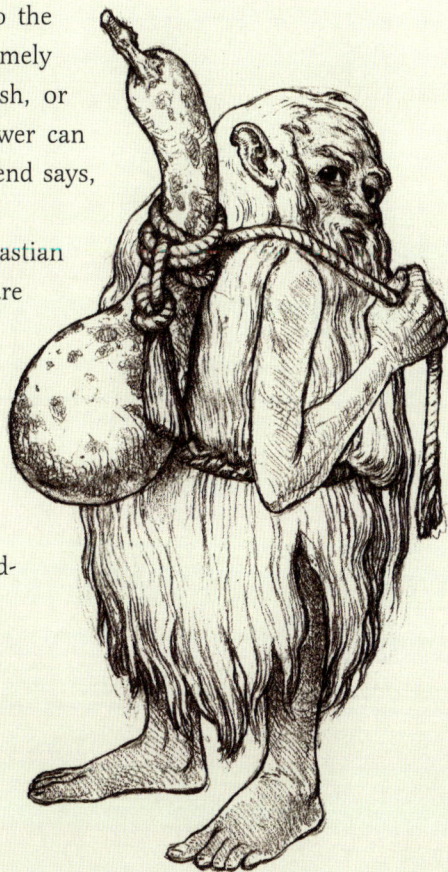

# THE GOOD FOLK

## CANADA

"The Good Folk" is the name given to fairies in many places around the world, including Canada, but especially Newfoundland. In fact, this is one area of the world where belief in fairy legends seems to have remained strong far into modern times. In Barbara Rieti's monograph on the subject, *Strange Terrain: The Fairy World in Newfoundland* (1991), she remarks that when she first came to Memorial University of Newfoundland in 1982 and saw their Folklore and Language Archive, she was "astonished" to find "hundreds of accounts of the fairies and descriptions of associated custom and belief, recorded mostly by student collectors over the past twenty-five years."

The Canadian Good Folk are strongly associated with berries. Peter Narváez even goes so far as to designate berry grounds as particularly liminal space in Newfoundland folklore, the fairy's land, a place where one might easily be "led astray" (i.e. lost for a time). Narváez also rightly points out that stories of being "led astray" by the fairies "may have provided culturally acceptable justifications for deviance, thereby extricating participants from embarrassing situations and potential shame." So, basically, a teenage girl's story about going out berry picking and being led astray by the fairies for a few hours makes a pretty good cover story for sneaking away and making out with her boyfriend. That's a fairly lighthearted example, but stories like this can also serve as ways of talking about far more sinister things as well, things too painful or stigmatizing to talk about directly, like rape and assault.

Should you decide to go out to pick berries, legend says you should do so with care and caution, because you do not want to upset these fairies. If you cross them, Anna Claybourne writes, you might get "hit with a 'fairy blast,' leaving you with a strange injury. Just when you think it's starting to heal, string, twigs, and fish bones will fall out of it!" They might also send winds and thunder to thwart humans or get them off their land. "To avoid all this, carry bread in your pockets, and wear your hat or jacket inside out. This confuses the fairies, and they'll leave you alone," Claybourne suggests. It's worth noting that the idea of the "fairy blast" is also very present in Scottish folklore, and it likely traveled with immigrants to Canada from the UK.

# MUKI

## ANDES MOUNTAINS, SOUTH AMERICA

The muki is a small goblin- or gnomelike creature who haunts the Andes Mountains. He lives underground, dwelling and working in the mines. He's often less than two feet tall, but very muscular, with long blond hair and a long beard, no neck, large feet, pale skin, and eyes that glimmer like the metals they seek in the mines. He also may have horns, which he can use to smash the rocks in his quest for precious metals. He usually wears mining gear, and may carry a lantern or wear a poncho or be clad in green from head to toe.

According to Jordan Faries, the word "muki" comes from the Quechuan, an indigenous family of languages, and "people in the Moquegua region in the south of Peru speak of a chinchiliku, and those in the northern Cajamarca region call it the jusshi."

As Anna Claybourne tells us, the muki is a truly amoral fairy. He sometimes steals tools and makes strange noises to frighten nearby humans, but other times he'll instead show people the best places to look for the metal in the mines (but only if they promise to keep the location a secret!). Break your word at your peril. If a human blabs about their meeting with the muki, the fairy might take revenge by collapsing a mining tunnel on top of them!

# POLEVOI/POLUDNITSA

## SLAVIC COUNTRIES

The polevoi, sometimes written as polevyk or poliovyk, is a Slavic field spirit. He watches over the field and protects it from those who don't respect it. Natalie Kononenko observes that "he punishes those who do not observe the proper prayers and sacrifices before going to work in the field."

The polevoi doesn't work alone, though. His female counterpart, called the poludnitsa, also "helps," and you'll understand the scare quotes momentarily. The poludnitsa is the spirit of the noontime, of the hottest part of the day, when the sun is at its roasting ascendency. The poludnitsa's job is to make sure that people are resting during this period instead of continuing to work in the field. Should they be foolish enough to attempt it, she attacks them while they work, striking them down with heatstroke or sunstroke.

While they're not the friendliest or most delightful fairies to encounter, they embody agricultural conventions and even safety measures. Their lore suggests it's wisest not only to respect the land but also to respect the need to rest and the limitations of the human body.

# ABATWA

## SOUTHERN AFRICA

Zulu folktales offer us a glimpse of some of the tiniest fairies in the world, the abatwa, otherwise known as the Zulu fairy hunters . . . but the history of these fairies gets a little tricky when we really dig into it.

According to A. Werner, the first mention of these fairies in English was in missionary Henry Callaway's 1868 book *Nursery Tales, Traditions, and Histories of the Zulus*, which Callaway describes as collected from Zulu story-tellers and translated and presented in such a way as to be as true to the stories heard directly as possible. The description of the abatwa was collected from a storyteller named Umpengula Mbanda, who described them as beings to fear. Though they were small enough to be able to take shelter underneath single blades of grass and travel via flea, nearly invisible, they could also attack via tiny arrows tipped with deadly poison. Anna Claybourne adds that they hate to be told that they're small, so if you see one, it's purportedly best to wax poetic about how big they are and how you never could have missed spotting them.

Now, all of that said, the word "abatwa" can also refer to an Indigenous group in Africa that used to be called "Bushmen" in older texts, a group that does seem to have originally been related to another Indigenous group that was classified as a pigmy culture. Werner points out that, though Callaway wrote that the fairy abatwa were entirely different from the human abatwa, many of these Indigenous groups had an "uncanny reputation as sorcerers among other tribes, and it is quite likely that these and other clearly mythical accounts are really intended to apply to them." After speaking with Misty L. Bastian on the subject, we would argue that Callaway (likely using his British understanding of fairylore) did not comprehend the deep and interconnected history of the African peoples and how their interactions may have been encoded in these tales. Thus, we're inclined to believe Werner's interpretation that the Zulu informant did intend to refer to the actual people and not a romanticized "pixie" like Callaway thought. As the idea of them as fairies has

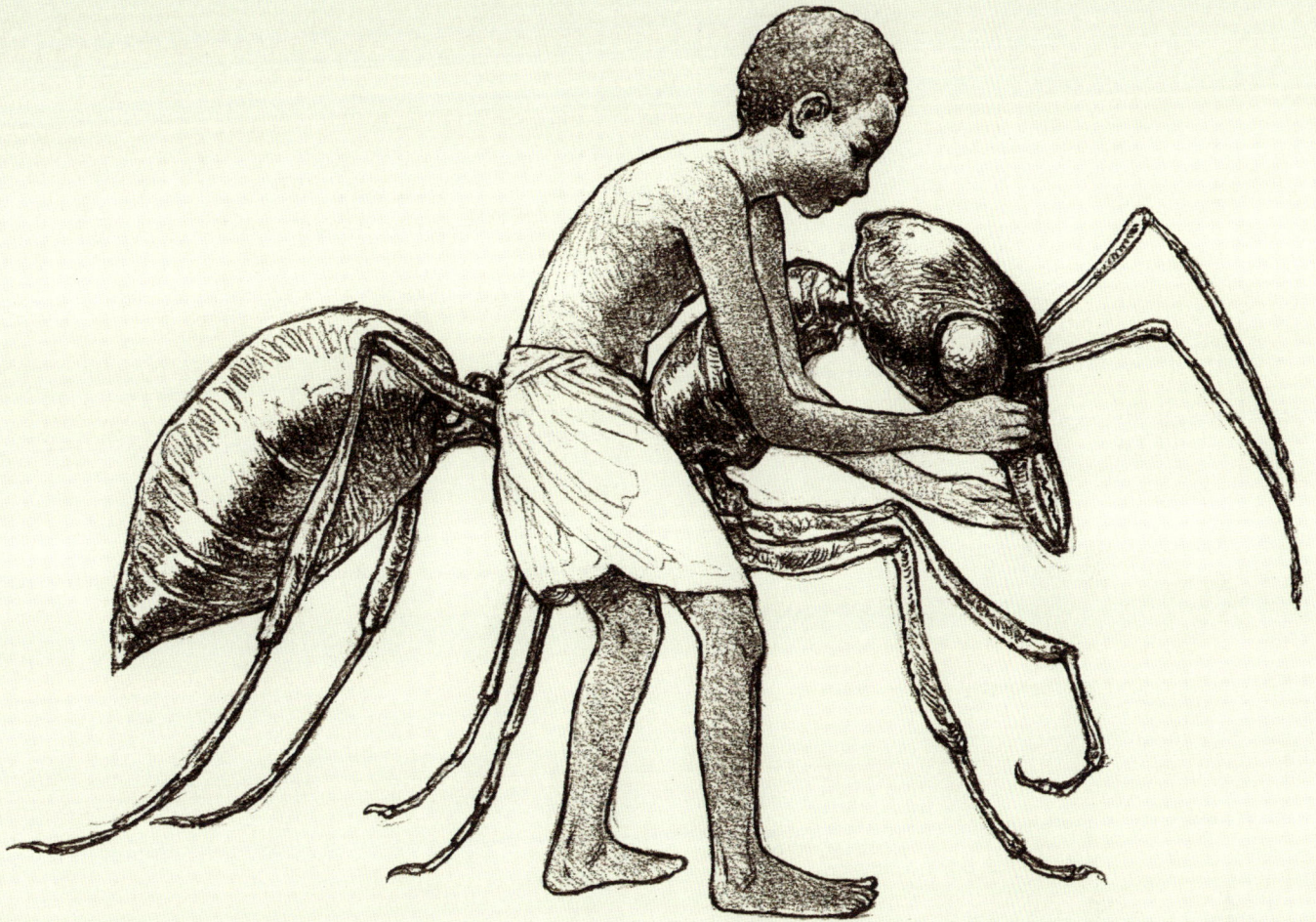

proliferated in the years since, we are including them here, but it's crucially important in this context to understand how this particular bit of folklore developed.

Bastian emphasizes that "the Abatwa fairies demand their due," that their true stature and potential impact must be recognized, lest disrespect be met with real strength, represented by their poisoned arrows, while at the same time "pixification" serves to underplay that power's potency. There are complex power dynamics at play, both the colonial and intertribal, here.

# MOOSLEUTE

## GERMANY

Moosleute translates as "Moss Folk," which is objectively one of the cutest things we've ever heard. These fairies hail from Southeastern Germany, primarily in the Bavarian forests. According to Thomas Keightley, they usually live in a society, but you can spot them on their own as well. Jacob Grimm himself speculated on their origins, gesturing to Greek and Norse connections, but later scholars point toward Old English and German etymologies instead. Timid and wary of humans, moosleute are intimately connected with trees and forest flora. They protect the trees of their forests, and they love to collect and weave the soft, beautiful moss that grows on tree roots and the surrounding ground. According to Anna Claybourne, they even "wear clothes of moss, and look like tiny trees themselves, with gnarled hands and long gray hair, like lichen." They're most often smaller than a human, sometimes beautiful, but sometimes shriveled and withered.

Moosleute can be slightly mischievous, too. If you've lost a key or a brush, perhaps it's been "borrowed" by one of these fairy folk. But in return, they've been known to do a good turn to the humans they encounter, whether by offering them bread or advice or by teaching them the medicinal properties of the forest plants they love. That said, the fairies of the wild hunt don't seem to be fond of them. Keightley tells a story where a peasant heard the sounds of a great hunt nearby and joined in with their cheering, not knowing it was anything supernatural. The "next morning he found hanging at his stable-door a quarter of a green Moss-woman as his share of the game," which, we imagine, was pretty horrifying!

# MIMI

## AUSTRALIA

The mimis are creatures of Indigenous Australian folklore, mainly found in central and northern Australia, particularly Arnhem Land. They dance through the colorful, energetic prehistoric rock paintings of the area, and legend has it that they might even have made these paintings themselves! Though the mimis have a humanoid shape, they're extremely slender and elongated. As Anna Claybourne points out, their fragile build makes them susceptible to damage from the elements, especially from strong winds. They tend to hide inside rocks to avoid this!

Mimis are said to have lived in Australia long before humans arrived, and are creatures of what Indigenous Australians refer as "the Dreaming." The Australian Museum describes "the Dreaming" or "Dreamtime" as "a complex network of knowledge, faith and practices that derive from stories of creation." It's a much more complicated idea than this, but you might think of it as a word for the mythic time before humans, when the supernatural was everywhere.

When the first people did appear in Australia, the mimis took on a mostly benevolent mentoring role, teaching humans how to hunt, paint, and make fire. Like most fairy creatures, though, they can also have a mischievous streak.

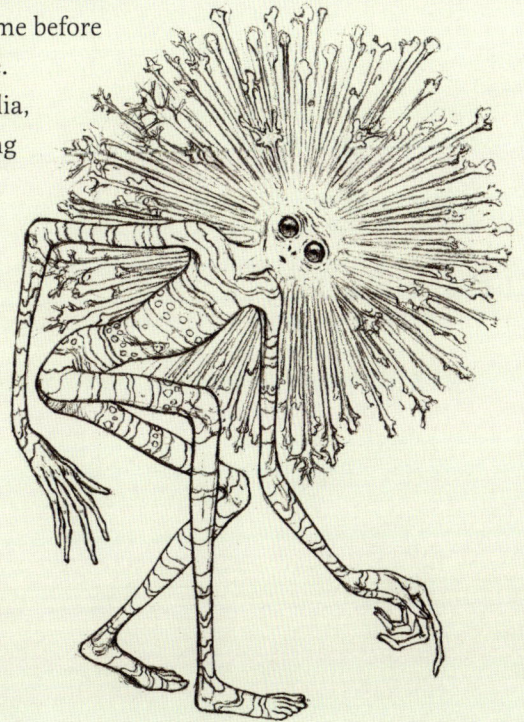

We'll be very up-front: Mermaids could be their own book. But they are basically the fairies of the sea, and it would feel odd to leave them out simply because they're aquatic and well known. We're painting with a very broad brush here because mermaid folklore is an absolutely massive category with a lot of variation, from Hans Christian Andersen's literary fairy tale "The Little Mermaid" to tales of Mami Wata found in parts of Africa and the Caribbean. To make matters even more complex, folklorist Katharine Briggs doesn't limit mermaids to the ocean, but includes fairies of lakes, ponds, and rivers as well. "The mermaids," she writes, "are perhaps of the most ambivalent character. The very sight of them at sea is death to sailors and it is their habit to decoy people under water, but at times they are benevolent, like the mermaid of Cury, who rewarded her rescuer with medical skill, and that in the Lowlands of Scotland, who rose in the water when a young girl's funeral was passing and lamented."

Almost every story about a mermaid is a love story. Of course, all kinds of fairies capture human hearts, but mermaids are especially entrenched in this tradition. And of course, they tend to end with heartbreak rather than a happily ever after. In folklore, mermaids are beautiful, dangerous, threatening, alluring, and completely impossible to hold on to. They can't be fully domesticated or integrated into human society. They're so like us, but they retain a wildness that makes them both incredibly alluring and profoundly incompatible in the long term.

# MERMAIDS

Though there are stories of murderous mermaids, they're not inherently sinister. They're as likely to rescue a drowning sailor as to spell doom for a ship just by existing nearby.

A mermaid can be a symbol of hope or destruction, but either way, she's something that can never be wholly known or controlled. Mermaids represent freedom from the rules and constraints of society, but that freedom comes at the steep cost of alienation and loss.

Scholars Christina Bacchilega and Marie Alohalani Brown understand that "our anxieties about water beings are magnified by our attraction to them, which in many stories results in the human's loss of control, self, and even life. Embracing a water spirit can prove lethal." While mermaids may frequently resemble beautiful humans from the waist up, beneath they are something else entirely. Bacchilega and Brown suggest that "there is something deeply unsettling about a being whose form merges the human with the nonhuman. Whether they dwell in fresh or salt water, aquatic humanoids raise questions about what it is to be human and what lies beyond a human centered world. Physically, they are both like and unlike us. They eat, sleep, and breathe in a realm that we can access only temporarily, but they can live among us, as they are often able to shed the nonhuman portion of their bodies and infiltrate the human world." Like love itself, mermaids can be at once familiar and strange, and it is perhaps this inherent distance that seems to make most mermaid stories of love so heartbreaking when they cannot stay.

# TROLL

## SCANDINAVIA

Trolls have experienced a bit of a cultural glow-up from their Norse mythological past. Where "troll" was once used to refer to an unsavory category that included evil spirits, large monsters, and sinister magic workers, the term no longer carries an especially malevolent connotation. In fact, they're more likely to be regarded as neutral or even positive. Unlike many fairies, they are not regarded as physically beautiful, but they are a lot nicer than many of the most stunning fairies, especially those lurking in the seduction chapter of this book.

Where to find a troll? Deep inside the earth. They live inside mountains, under hills, and within caves, where they might be solitary, part of a family, or part of an expansive and complex troll community.

Perhaps part of the reason they prefer homes underground is that they're thought to really hate loud noises. Thomas Keightley wrote that their aversion is "probably from a recollection of the time when Thor used to be flinging his hammer after them; so that the hanging of bells in churches has driven them almost all out of the country." Because of this, humans, especially in Nordic regions, have hung bells in defense when they are plagued by a wayward troll.

Despite the tension around bells, trolls are often friendly and helpful, and they may be willing to interact with humans in a neighborly sort of way rather than retreating into secrecy and concealment. However, there are also stories of them generally wreaking havoc, stealing valuables and even abducting women and children from nearby human settlements.

One of the most compelling things about trolls is that they're often described as profoundly *humanlike* in their actions and connections: Keightley tells us that "they marry, have children, bake and brew, just as the peasant himself does. A farmer one day met a bill-man and his wife, and a whole squad of stumpy little children, in his fields; and people used often to see the children of the man who lived in the hill of Kund, in Jutland, climbing up the hill, and rolling down after one another, with shouts of laughter."

Of course, they also have some distinctly superhuman tools at their disposal, too. Trolls are sometimes said to possess powers of invisibility and shapeshifting. Some stories tell of trolls with prophetic skills, or the power to bestow good or ill luck and even incredible strength upon others.

# YUNWI TSUNSDI

## CHEROKEE NATION

The yunwi tsunsdi are the "little people" of Cherokee nation folklore. They're small, humanoid nature spirits. Usually invisible to humans, they may choose to reveal themselves to people they want to help or hinder. In fact, according to John Witthoft and Wendell S. Hadlock, there are four kinds of yunwi tsunsdi: those that live in rock cliffs, those that live in laurel patches, those that live in the broom sage, and those that live out in the open. The broom sage variety and the ones that live out in the open are said to be very antisocial, while the rock cliff yunwi tsunsdi are kind.

The lore says to let them come to you instead of seeking them out. They might appear to rescue a lost human child, but they prefer to offer their aid on their own terms. They love playing tricks, and sometimes they even guard treasure. Show them disrespect or aggression at your peril. They're said to use their magic to punish people who mess with them. The yunwi tsunsdi wear their hair long, almost to the ground, and they love music, especially drumming, which is said to echo through the mountains and the forests of Cherokee lands. Anna Claybourne offers this reminder: "If you find something valuable on the ground, such as a necklace or a knife, you must politely ask the yunwi tsunsdi before you take it, in case it belongs to them."

# ORANG BUNIAN

## INDONESIA AND MALAYSIA

The orang bunian are similar to the Icelandic huldufólk in many ways. They also live up in mountains and deep in forests and jungles, but they function very similarly to humans otherwise. They are usually invisible, and only people with second sight can see them. If you do see them, however, they'll often appear to be "an old-fashioned human, but with a white, ghostly, foggy appearance," as Anna Claybourne puts it. We're definitely seeing echoes of ghosts here. Some say they live in a parallel world, which may be why, when they are spotted, they are seen as if through a veil. In fact, they may cause a kind of disorientation, especially on mountains (or at least they're blamed for that kind of thing). These fairies are usually fairly kind, but they have definitely been known to kidnap people on occasion, too. Jeffrey Hadler tells us that stories of orang bunian women luring away human men are still told today.

# TENGU

## JAPAN

The tengu, or mountain goblin, is a mischievous creature from Japanese folklore. They're one of the best known of all yōkai and are culturally iconic throughout Japan. Tengu are birdlike in appearance, and their martial arts skills are unparalleled. According to folklorist Michael Dylan Foster, they're "often associated with Buddhism and mountain ascetic practices. Even today, there are mountain shrines and festivals that honor Tengu." Tengu are sometimes believed to be reincarnated spirits, especially of people who were proud or arrogant during their human lives.

There are two distinct varieties of tengu. The karasu tengu, or "crow tengu," is especially birdlike. It has wings, a beak, and the ability to fly, and is often depicted as a bird of prey. However, during the Edo period, these karasu tengu culturally gave way to a new tengu, one that, while still avian, was also much more human in form. These new tengu were tall and wore the garb of a Buddhist monk or other local religious figures. They also had long, pronounced, and very red noses. This is the version of the tengu that has really stuck, but occasionally you'll see this tengu surrounded by karasu tengu minions, who lurk at his disposal.

Despite all the wings, beaks, and general bird accoutrements, "tengu" actually translates as "celestial dog" or "heavenly hound," but they never look or act like dogs in the folklore. Why are these bird fairies named after dogs? We wish we could tell you. Foster says: "It is impossible to unpack the exact process by which a word meaning 'heavenly hound' and indicating an astronomical occurrence gradually came to signify a long-nosed monk with wings, but it is clear that this transmogrification reflects a mixture of historical, religious, and popular influences. For example, the avian image of the Tengu may be associated in some way with the Garuda, a deific bird figure that features prominently in both Hindu and Buddhist beliefs, and which most likely entered Japan through China—along with Buddhism itself."

The cultural meaning and weight of the tengu have really shifted over time. In the Heian period, they were regarded as mysterious and malignant creatures likely to inflict illness or to generally mess with the humans they encountered. At this time, their appearance lacked much continuity. These tengu might be invisible, avian, or humanoid. The Kamakura period ushered in a more static vision of the tengu. Foster tells us that they were "considered after-death incarnations of emperors of dead warriors, they would appear as malevolent birdlike creatures, monks, or *yamabushi* (mountain ascetics), descending from the mountains to torment the powers that be." Around the twelfth century, the association between the tengu and Buddhism grew stronger, especially through the concept of ma, or the evil force that tampers with the pursuit of enlightenment. However, over time, the tengu proved themselves to be more morally ambiguous than outright evil.

They've even become a beloved symbol of rebellion and resistance. Foster explains, "We can also imagine how Tengu might become potent symbols of the underdog, representing a rebellious, antiauthoritarian spirit. It is perhaps in this context that they became famous for knowing secret martial arts techniques. Most famously, it is said that tengu trained Minamoto no Yoshitsune, one of the great warriors of Japanese history."

# Story of a Tengu

*Retold by Lafcadio Hearn*

## JAPAN

Lafcadio Hearn's "Story of a Tengu" displays the nature of this
particular fairy perfectly—all the crucial details are there. Further, the
significant engagement between the fairy creature and the human
makes it a perfect example story for this chapter.

In the days of the Emperor Go-Reizei, there
was a holy priest living in the temple of Saito,
on the mountain called Hiyei-Zan, near Kyōto.
One summer day this good priest, after a visit to the city, was returning to his temple by
way of Kita-no-Ōji, when he saw some boys
ill-treating a kite. They had caught the bird in a
snare, and were beating it with sticks. "Oh, the
poor creature!" compassionately exclaimed
the priest;—"why do you torment it so, children?" One of the boys made answer:—"We
want to kill it to get the feathers." Moved by
pity, the priest persuaded the boys to let him
have the kite in exchange for a fan that he was
carrying; and he set the bird free. It had not
been seriously hurt, and was able to fly away.

Happy at having performed this Buddhist
act of merit, the priest then resumed his walk.
He had not proceeded very far when he saw

a strange monk come out of a bamboo-grove
by the road-side, and hasten towards him. The
monk respectfully saluted him, and said:—"Sir,
through your compassionate kindness my life
has been saved; and I now desire to express
my gratitude in a fitting manner." Astonished
at hearing himself thus addressed, the priest
replied:—"Really, I cannot remember to have
ever seen you before: please tell me who you
are." "It is not wonderful that you cannot recognize me in this form," returned the monk:
"I am the kite that those cruel boys were tormenting at Kita-no-Ōji. You saved my life; and
there is nothing in this world more precious
than life. So I now wish to return your kindness in some way or other. If there be anything
that you would like to have, or to know, or to
see,—anything that I can do for you, in short,—
please to tell me; for as I happen to possess, in

和州西嚴寺古閑筆

TENGU ON BOAR. FROM A DRAWING
BY KOKAN, ENGRAVED IN THE WA-KAN MEI-HITSU
KINGIOKU GWA-FU (1771), FROM *JAPANESE
WOOD ENGRAVINGS: THEIR HISTORY,
TECHNIQUE AND CHARACTERISTICS*

a small degree, the Six Supernatural Powers, I am able to gratify almost any wish that you can express." On hearing these words, the priest knew that he was speaking with a Tengu; and he frankly made answer:—"My friend, I have long ceased to care for the things of this world: I am now seventy years of age; neither fame nor pleasure has any attraction for me. I feel anxious only about my future birth; but as that is a matter in which no one can help me, it were useless to ask about it. Really, I can think of but one thing worth wishing for. It has been my life-long regret that I was not in India in the time of the Lord Buddha, and could not attend the great assembly on the holy mountain Gridhrakûta. Never a day passes in which this regret does not come to me, in the hour of morning or of evening prayer. Ah, my friend! if it were possible to conquer Time and Space, like the Bodhisattvas, so that I could look upon that marvellous assembly, how happy should I be!"

"Why," the Tengu exclaimed, "that pious wish of yours can easily be satisfied. I perfectly well remember the assembly on the Vulture Peak; and I can cause everything that happened there to reappear before you, exactly as it occurred. It is our greatest delight to represent such holy matters. . . . Come this way with me!"

And the priest suffered himself to be led to a place among pines, on the slope of a hill. "Now," said the Tengu, "you have only to wait here for awhile, with your eyes shut. Do not open them until you hear the voice of the Buddha preaching the Law. Then you can look. But when you see the appearance of the Buddha, you must not allow your devout feelings to influence you in any way;—you must not bow down, nor pray, nor utter any such exclamation as, *'Even so, Lord!'* or *'O thou Blessed One!'* You must not speak at all. Should you make even the least sign of reverence, something very unfortunate might happen to me." The priest gladly promised to follow these injunctions; and the Tengu hurried away as if to prepare the spectacle.

The day waned and passed, and the darkness came; but the old priest waited patiently beneath a tree, keeping his eyes closed. At last a voice suddenly resounded above him,—a wonderful voice, deep and clear like the pealing of a mighty bell,—the voice of the Buddha Sâkyamuni proclaiming the Perfect Way. Then the priest, opening his eyes in a great radiance,

perceived that all things had been changed: the place was indeed the Vulture Peak,—the holy Indian mountain Gridhrakûta; and the time was the time of the Sûtra of the Lotos of the Good Law. Now there were no pines about him, but strange shining trees made of the Seven Precious Substances, with foliage and fruit of gems;—and the ground was covered with Mandârava and Manjûshaka flowers showered from heaven;—and the night was filled with fragrance and splendour and the sweetness of the great Voice. And in mid-air, shining as a moon above the world, the priest beheld the Blessed One seated upon the Lion-throne, with Samantabhadra at his right hand, and Mañjusrî at his left,—and before them assembled—immeasurably spreading into Space, like a flood Of stars—the hosts of the Mahâsattvas and the Bodhisattvas with their countless following: "gods, demons, Nâgas, goblins, men, and beings not human." Sâriputra he saw, and Kâsyapa, and Ânanda, with all the disciples of the Tathâgata,—and the Kings of the Devas,—and the Kings of the Four Directions, like pillars of fire,—and the great Dragon-Kings,—and the Gandharvas and Garudas,—and the Gods of the Sun and the Moon and the Wind,—and the shining myriads of Brahmâ's heaven. And incomparably further than even the measureless circling of the glory of these, he saw—made visible by a single ray of light that shot from the forehead of the Blessed One to pierce beyond uttermost Time—the eighteen hundred thousand Buddha-fields of the Eastern Quarter with all their habitants,—and the beings in each of the Six States of Existence,—and even the shapes of the Buddhas extinct, that had entered into Nirvâna. These, and all the gods, and all the demons, he saw bow down before the Lion-throne; and he heard that multitude incalculable of beings praising the Sûtra of the Lotos of the Good Law,—like the roar of a sea before the Lord. Then forgetting utterly his pledge,—foolishly dreaming that he stood in the very presence of the very Buddha,—he cast himself down in worship with tears of love and thanksgiving; crying out with a loud voice, "O thou Blessed One!" . . .

Instantly with a shock as of earthquake the stupendous spectacle disappeared; and the priest found himself alone in the dark, kneeling upon the grass of the mountain-side.

Then a sadness unspeakable fell upon him, because of the loss of the vision, and because of the thoughtlessness that had caused him to break his word. As he sorrowfully turned his steps homeward, the goblin-monk once more appeared before him, and said to him in tones of reproach and pain:—"Because you did not keep the promise which you made to me, and heedlessly allowed your feelings to overcome you, the Gōhotendo, who is the Guardian of the Doctrine, swooped down suddenly from heaven upon us, and smote us in great anger, crying out, 'How do ye dare thus to deceive a pious person?' Then the other monks, whom I had assembled, all fled in fear. As for myself, one of my wings has been broken,—so that now I cannot fly." And with these words the Tengu vanished forever.

CHAPTER 6

# OUR FAIRIES, OURSELVES

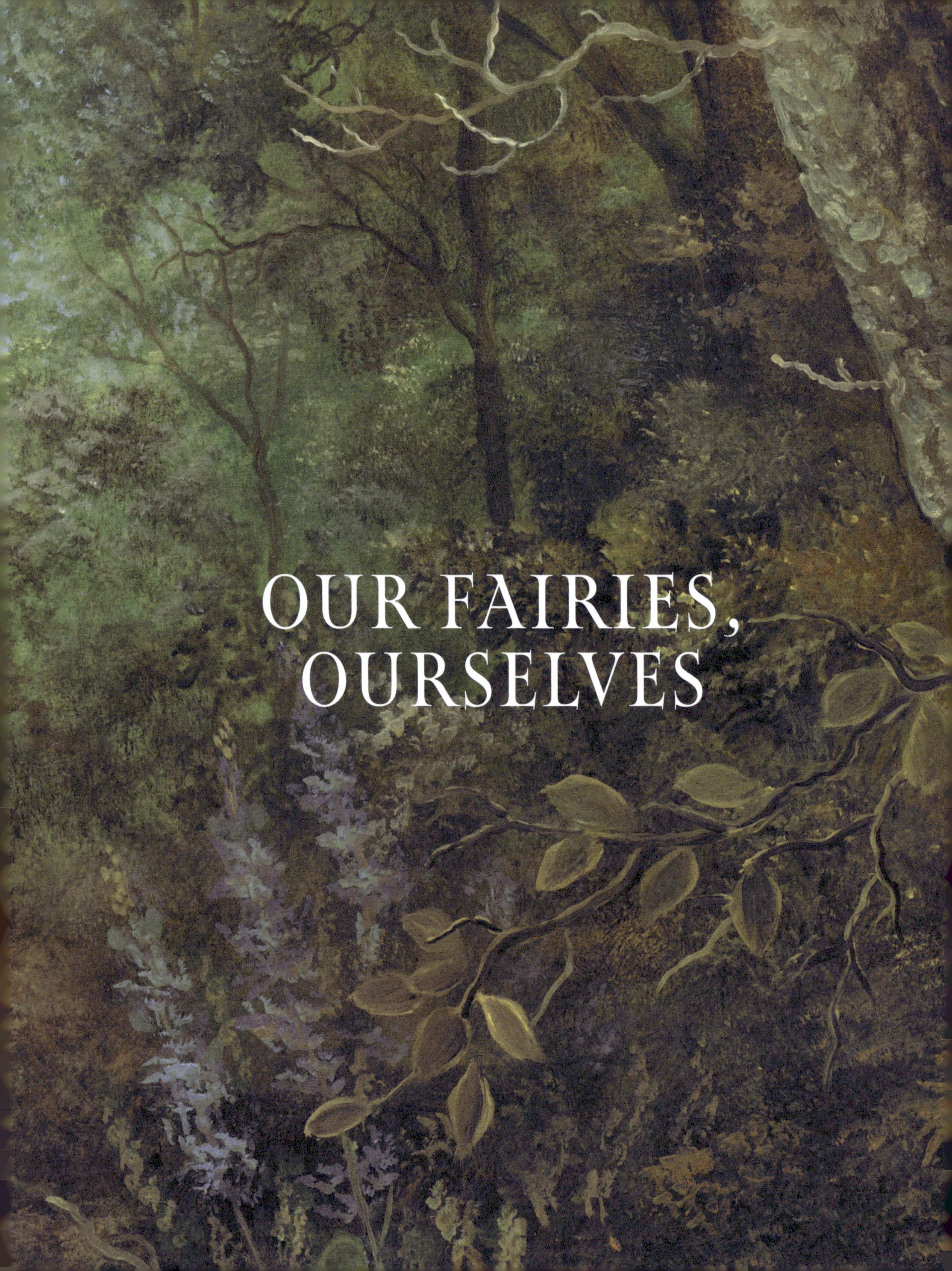

This chapter tackles the places where the boundaries blur between fairy and human. The best example of this is probably the wealth of changeling lore—stories of human children and fairies that are swapped—that can be found all over the world. As Katharine Briggs points out, the stories of fairies typically "make it clear that they are not generally conceived of as existing in an independent and self-contained state, but have great concern with mortal things. [. . .] However happily they may seem to pass their days in feasting and riding and the delights of music, however much they resent human spying or human interference, they are never thought of as indifferent to men; human help is necessary to many of their activities, and they greatly desire to influence human destiny." In fact, she adds, "they work and play and fight and dance and hunt, but it sometimes seems doubtful if they are doing more than acting over what they have seen humans do, or anticipating human happenings and disasters." With this in mind, here we'll take on the changeling, fairy doctors and midwives, Icelandic elf-women who steal children, a few famous humans who teeter on the edge of fairyhood, and more. These are the fairies who are, in a sense, *us*.

# CHANGELINGS

A changeling is a fairy creature that mimics the human form for sinister purposes, after the actual human in question, usually a child, has been abducted by other fairies.

However, "changeling" can mean a lot of other things, too. While a changeling may be the fairy that is left in place of an abducted human, "changeling" could also be a way to refer to the *human* that was stolen away. In cases of abduction, fairies may leave behind objects or detritus enchanted to look like the stolen child, and that enchantment may *also* be referred to as a changeling. The changeling umbrella might also include children that result from a human-fairy sexual relationship. These children are often said to have some kind of marked physical difference, like webbed hands or striking coloration, ostensibly so that the fairy parent would be able to recognize the child as their own so they could take it back to Faerie with them. The word "changeling" gets a lot of mileage in a variety of supernatural circumstances. Almost anything involved in a fairy abduction can qualify.

As Joyce Underwood Munro reminds us, the changeling tradition is widespread throughout much of Europe and also appears in Egypt, India, China, and the Pacific Northwest. This means that there's really no one way for changelings to look or behave. That said, there do seem to be certain characteristics that show up again and again.

For instance, a changeling may be identifiable by his monstrous appetite. No matter how much he eats, he's never full, and he may hunger for inedible materials that no human could ever consider to be food. Regardless of how much he eats, he remains thin, undersized, and sickly. Most often, he's considered quite small for his age. In general, changelings are described as wizened, with wrinkled skin regardless of age. A changeling may also have misshapen limbs, an unusually large head, and trouble or slowness when walking. They may avoid walking, running, or dancing unless they think no one is watching. Some traditions suggest that a changeling rarely sings, smiles, or talks, but they may cry at great length and volume. When they do speak, a changeling may speak in fairy riddles, much to the confusion of his

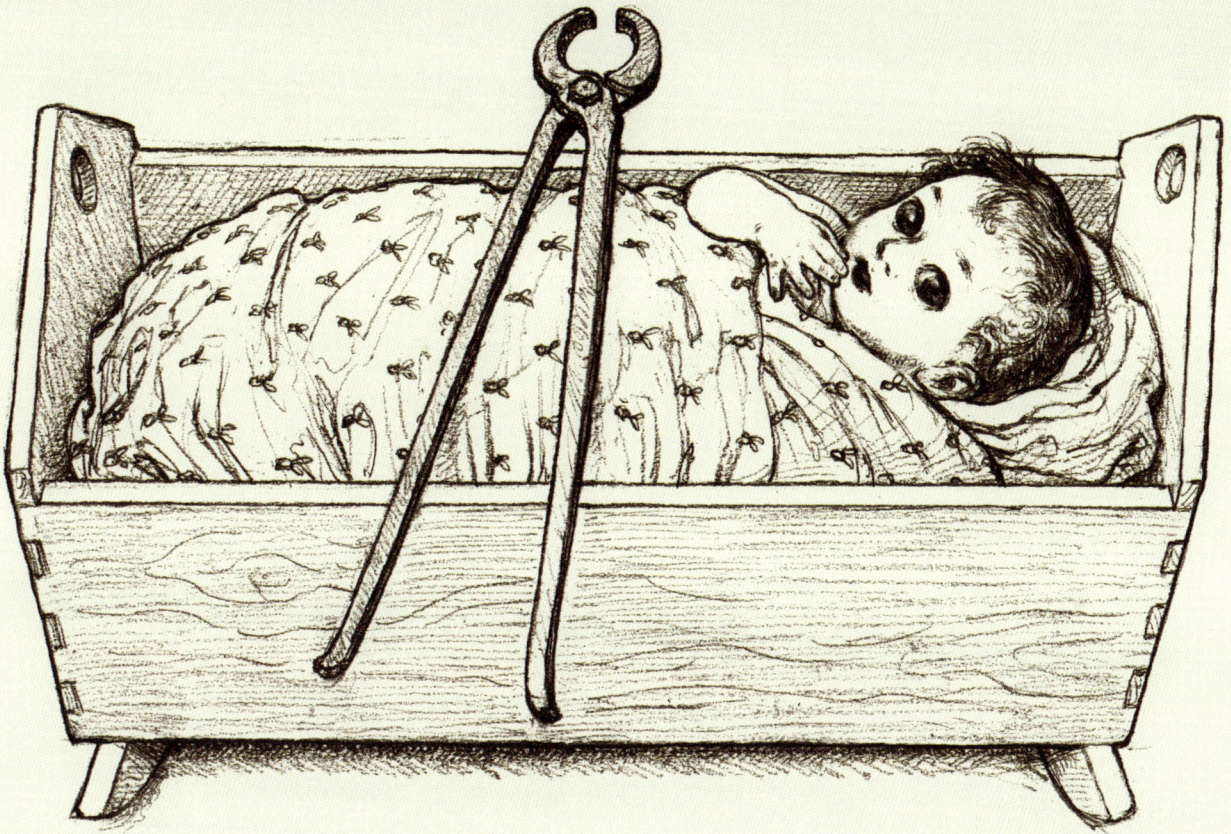

family. According to Munro, a changeling might reveal himself through "a bizarre cooking exercise [. . .], playing the bagpipes, or calculating the age of the forest." Susan Schoon Eberly adds that changelings are also more often, though not always, boys.

While most changeling tales are about the changelings already living among humans, there are occasional stories about an attempted abduction being thwarted by determined parents. For instance, Wirt Sikes shares a tale of this kind: "Dazzy Walter, the wife of Abel Walter, of Ebwy Fawr, one night in her husband's absence awoke in her bed and found her baby was not at her side. In great fright she sought for it, and caught it with her hand upon the boards above the bed, which was as far as the fairies had succeeded in carrying it."

As stories like this imply, there are strategies to prevent fairies from making off with your child and leaving a changeling in its place. Piety is sometimes believed to be preventative. So is putting a knife in your child's cradle or placing a pair of tongs across it whenever you leave them unattended. In Christian contexts, baptism is often thought to be the most effective prevention you could offer, but laying a Bible under the child's pillow might also help. Sikes adds, hilariously, that in places ranging from Scotland to China, hanging the father's breeches on the wall is considered an effective strategy. We say "hilariously," but this is also pretty sexist, no? It implies that the mother alone wouldn't be able to fend off a fairy abduction, or that fairies would only respect the man of the house. Come on, fairies, be better!

Finally, we want to talk about something pretty important regarding the way that changeling stories have been used in the past. These fairies are among the most beloved, frequently invoked fairies out there. In many ways, they're used symbolically to represent outsider status or the feeling of not fitting in. But the history of changeling tales is complex, and changeling lore has been used to marginalize those who are different.

"Changeling" invokes not only the supernatural but disability. They're often associated with ill-health, strangeness, and liminality. Scholars like Eberly and Munro have argued that, among other possibilities, changeling narratives developed as a way to explain things like central nervous system disorders, cerebral palsy, Down syndrome, Hunter's or Hurler's syndrome, and many other things that result in physical and developmental differences in babies and children. These scholars have explicitly connected stories of changelings to descriptions of congenital disorders or ill health. Eberly points out that changelings are frequently described as "the infant or very young child who is different, whether that difference arises through injury, disease, or congenital disorder and there are times [. . .] when the record is clear enough to suggest a fairly clear relationship between the child described and a known disorder." In fact, Eberly argues that many kinds of fairies, not just changelings, have been used to explain "congenital disorders," and that "there are a number of fairy characters—the changeling, the solitary fairies, and the child of the human-fairy parentage—who seem to [. . .] clearly represent certain congenital disorders. [. . .] The different child who survives, perhaps with more mental than physical difference, offers a rational explanation for many of the solitary fairies." She goes on to explain that blaming fairies for disability has historically been a strategy to remove social blame for those things from a child's mother. In other words, if a child was different, a family could blame that difference on the fairies instead of the mother's evil or impure thoughts or on divine vengeance or retribution for sin, as was, unfortunately, not an uncommon occurrence.

These "changeling" children are heavily othered, described as diabolical, disagreeable, and frightening. Sikes adds that, sometimes, they are described as having notably dark skin, using race as another way to differentiate them from their families. And while some families and communities embraced the people they'd identified as changelings, such a label could also provoke horrific violence. Speaking specifically about changeling stories from Wales, Sikes writes:

> Under the pretense of proving whether the objectionable baby
> is a changeling or not, it is held on a shovel over the fire, or it
> is bathed in a solution of the fox-glove, which kills it; a case
> where this test was applied is said to have actually occurred
> in Carnarvonshire in 1857. That there is nothing especially
> Welsh in this, needs not be pointed out. Apart from the fact that
> infanticide, like murder, is of no country, similar practices as to
> changelings have prevailed in most European lands, either to test
> the child's uncanny quality, or, that being admitted, to drive it
> away and thus compel the fairies to restore the missing infant. In
> Denmark the mother heats the oven, and places the changeling
> on the peel, pretending to put it in; or whips it severely with a
> rod; or throws it into the water. In Sweden they employ similar
> methods. In Ireland the hot shovel is used.

The changeling is a powerful figure representing ostracization and violence but also a metaphor for expressing marginalized identities. Today, some disabled people, especially those on the autism spectrum, reclaim the concept of changelings as a way to illustrate their neurodivergent experiences, adding another chapter to the changeling's story. But even so, there's no denying that this is a piece of folklore heavily tainted by a history of violence and intolerance.

Once upon a time, in 1917, two young girls, Frances Griffiths (age ten) and Elsie Wright (age thirteen), used a small camera to take pictures of the fairies they said they saw in the woods near Elsie's home in Cottingley, England. Later, when Elsie's father developed the photographs, he thought they must have been faked somehow, probably with paper cutouts, but he couldn't find any real evidence, so he didn't think much more of it. A few years later, in 1920, Elsie's mother heard a lecture about spirit photography and gave the lecturer, Dr. Edward Gardner, her daughter's negatives. He then gave them to a professional photographer, Harold Snelling, who did *not* think they were faked. Fascinated, Gardner then took them to Kodak itself, who couldn't prove they were faked either. Soon after this, Sir Arthur Conan Doyle—yes, *that* Sir Arthur Conan Doyle, of Sherlock Holmes fame—wrote an article where he stated that he, too, believed that the photos were real images of real fairies.

But were they? Well, let's just quote what Katharine Briggs said about their verisimilitude: "Against it any folklorist puts up a very strong aesthetic resistance; for these fairies seem the very model of the butterfly-winged, gauze-clad fairies of the children's magazine illustrations." And, of course, it did turn out that they were not real . . . or at least most of them were not. The fifth and last photograph, the most realistic of the bunch, does still make people ponder, not least because Frances went to her grave claiming that that one was the one true image.

To us, this story clearly shows one of the ways that fairies are still incredibly powerful in our world. As Richard Sugg argues in his article on the images, "Fairy Magic and The Cottingley Photographs," England was just coming out of World War I, and its ghosts were still felt everywhere. Many people, Doyle included, had lost loved ones and longed to see some kind of magic in the world again. In 1983, Elsie would even admit that she had felt sorry for Doyle, who clearly wanted to believe so much. The photographs gave those people something important, something perhaps even more important than the so-called truth.

# THE COTTINGLEY FAIRIES

# THE GREEN CHILDREN

## ENGLAND, UK

The legend of the Green Children tells of two seemingly feral children who were found near the village of Woolpit in Suffolk, England, in the twelfth century. Their name comes from their skin, which was an unearthly pale green. When they were found, they didn't seem to understand human language—they were said to instead speak an unfamiliar language that was incomprehensible to the locals—and they seemed terrified and confused. They refused most human food but ate raw broad beans ravenously. Their diet did eventually expand, but despite this, the boy faded away and died. His sister survived and integrated, at least somewhat, into human society. She learned to speak the local tongue, and her skin lost its green tinge. According to Katharine Briggs, when pressed on their past, the girl said that she and her brother had "lived in an underground country, where there was neither sun nor moon but a soft light like twilight." The girl did grow up and get married, but Briggs notes that she "was always rather free and wanton in her behavior," refusing to fully relinquish her fairy wildness or submit to the conventions of the time. The earliest known stories of the Green Children were published in William of Newburgh's *Historia rerum Anglicarum* (ca. 1189) and Ralph of Coggeshall's *Chronicum Anglicanum* (ca. 1220). After that, few mentions of them appeared for hundreds of years, but a revived fascination with them developed in the 1800s, giving new life to the legend and inviting speculation on just how close a fairy realm might be to the human world.

# FAIRY DOCTORS / CUNNING FOLK

In addition to changelings, many human beings of all ages have been caught up in the fairy world in one way or another. One of the most common ways, at least in Celtic areas, was to become what was known there as a member of the cunning folk, or even a "fairy doctor." These were the people you would go to if you were afflicted with some strange disease, some ailment you couldn't explain, or if you feared your son or daughter might be falling in love with a malicious fairy. Basically fairy doctors would, it was said, know what to do if you had any kind of suspected entanglement with the fairies. A lawyer from Cornwall, who chose to remain anonymous, told W. Y. Evans-Wentz that "Jimmy Thomas, of Wendron parish, who died within the last twenty-five years, was the last witch-doctor I know about in West Cornwall. He was supposed to have great power over evil spirits. His immediate predecessor was a woman, called the 'Witch of Wendron', and she did big business." Apparently you could make a pretty good living off this kind of thing if you knew what you were doing! Fairy doctors often claimed to have abilities like second sight (the ability to see fairies), could sometimes talk to the fairies and get insights directly from them, and may have even been to the world of the fairies themselves at some point in their life.

In fact, coming up with a story about being gifted with your abilities by the fairies was one of the safer ways to engage with any power that could be deemed supernatural. Diane Purkiss notes that "fairies were less intimidating and less culpable than the devil; yet they were not beings with whom most early moderns felt at ease. Stories about fairies created awe without terrifying the client away." Even "more sophisticated magicians—magicians with a university education—also conjured fairies, or spirits with fairy names at least." That said, it's important to remember that any human connection to magic was a potentially dangerous gift to have. It would be all too easy to accuse a fairy doctor of demonic witchcraft if they failed to help you or angered you in some way!

Morgan le Fay is an ambiguous, mysterious figure in traditional Arthurian legend. In many of the oldest texts, she serves as the good woman (and sometimes sister) who arrives at the end of King Arthur's life to take him to Avalon. Often she appears as his wild and unknowable enemy, a wicked sorceress obsessed with destroying Camelot however she can. Remarkably, she can even be both in the same text. However she appears, she's heavily associated with magic and, more specifically, with fairies. In fact, she's often a half fairy herself, the daughter of a mortal and a fairy, making her an interesting test case to think through the fate of half-fairy children and changelings.

Her first known appearance is in *La Vita Merlini* (ca. 1150) by Geoffrey of Monmouth, in which he writes:

> There nine sisters rule by a pleasing set of laws those who come to them from our country. She who is first of them is more skilled in the healing art, and excels her sisters in the beauty of her person. Morgen is her name, and she has learned what useful properties all the herbs contain, so that she can cure sick bodies. She also knows an art by which to change her shape, and to cleave the air on new wings like Daedalus [. . .] and when she will she slips down from the air onto your shores. And men say that she has taught mathematics to her sisters.

(You can tell she's definitely magical because *girl math*.)

In this early appearance, she seems pretty benevolent, but over time, her reputation took a massive hit. According to Charlotte Spivack, in "the French prose romances [. . .] her character changes dramatically. She degenerates in both her purposes and in her powers, becoming a malicious master of black arts." By the time Sir Thomas Malory wrote his famous version of the Arthurian legend, *Le Morte D'arthur*, in 1485, Morgan le Fay had entered her villainous era.

MORGAN LE FAY

# FAIRY MIDWIVES / NURSING MOTHERS

You've already read of changelings and the high value of human children to fairies, but human babies are not the only vulnerable group where fairy abduction is concerned. Midwives and nursing mothers are also said to be extremely tempting to fairies, as fairies seem to struggle with low birth rates. Thus these women represent another category of humanity that gets entangled with the fairies more often than they might like.

In UK and Irish stories, Briggs tells us that "the human midwife is almost as important to the fairies as the nursing mother, it seems sometimes as if fairy babies could not be delivered without human aid." She adds that "next to unchristened children, nursing mothers who had not yet been churched were in the greatest danger. These were carried away into Fairyland to give suck to fairy babies." A nursing mother's milk is seen as valuable not only as a source of nutrition but also as a way to infuse a newborn fairy with a soul. Remember, one of the common themes in fairylore is that fairies lack a mortal soul and thus can't get to heaven. These abducted women, whether for midwifery or nursing purposes, do often get one solid perk though: an ointment to put on their eyes that will gift them with fairy sight.

W. Y. Evans-Wentz also relays this fairy midwife story from Mary Owen and Betsy Thomas of Wales:

> [A] farmer went to Llangefni to fetch a woman to nurse his wife
> about to become a mother, and he found one of the *Tylwyth Teg*,
> who came with him on the back of his horse. Arrived at the
> farm-house, the fairy woman looked at the wife, and giving the
> farmer some oil told him to wash his baby in it as soon as it was
> born. Then the fairy woman disappeared. The farmer followed
> the advice, and what did he do in washing the baby but get some
> oil on one of his own eyes. Suddenly he could see the *Tylwyth Teg*,
> for the oil had given him the second-sight. Some time later the

farmer was in Llangefni again, and saw the same fairy woman who had given him the oil. "How is your wife getting on?" she asked him. "She is getting on very well," he replied. Then the fairy woman added, "Tell me with which eye you see the best." "With this one," he said, pointing to the eye he had rubbed with the oil. And the fairy woman put her stick in that eye, and the farmer never saw with it again.

Apparently that whole second sight thing may sometimes be just a temporary, and very dangerous, gift. As Evans-Wentz notes, a midwife being an actual fairy herself is pretty rare. In fact, this is the only midwife tale he found in North Wales. Mostly the stories are human women being taken to tend to fairy children instead of the other way around!

This is admittedly a bit of a tricky one, since Robert Kirk isn't a fairy . . . or is he? Legend suggests that he became a fairy or maybe was of Faerie all along, so let's discuss.

Robert Kirk was a minister and scholar in seventeenth-century Scotland. We might even call him a proto-folklorist, though folklore was neither a discipline nor a recognized word when Kirk was alive. As folklorists, though, we love that early fairy-tale scholar Andrew Lang refers to Kirk as more of "an early student in folk-lore and in psychical research" than anything else, someone who was fascinated by his subject and not immediately dismissive or overly superstitious about it. In fact, Lang says, "he treats his matter in a scientific spirit, as if he were dealing with generally recognized physical phenomena."

Kirk was a seventh son and a student of theology at St. Andrews, and he worked in Balquhidder and then Aberfoyle in Scotland. He died (maybe) in 1692.

So why are we writing about him here? Well, after he died, legends sprang up saying that he wasn't really *dead*-dead but that the fairies had stolen him away because he had revealed too many of their secrets. Kirk's fame is the result of those legends and also because of a treatise that he wrote called *The Secret Commonwealth* (1691), which explored the Scottish supernatural landscape, including fairy folklore, ghosts, magic, and second sight (the ability to see fairies and other supernatural phenomena). This work remained unpublished for over a hundred years, until another Scottish author, Sir Walter Scott, released it in 1815. In 1893, Lang compiled the most definitive edition of the book, expanding the title to *The Secret Commonwealth of Elves, Fauns and Fairies*. Lang called this book "a kind of metaphysic of the Fairy world."

In *The Secret Commonwealth*, Kirk writes of second sight as the ability to see fairies and fairy objects for what they really are. For Kirk, this gift also grants the ability to see the outcome of future events, a kind of prophetic bonus to true seeing. And he really doubles down on this. As R. J. Stewart puts it, "Kirk affirms the Second Sight and the existence of the Fairy Race, using all the

ROBERT KIRK

scholarly logical and philosophical techniques, citations and arguments at his disposal to do so." Stewart argues that "Kirk wrote this short book not as a 'folklore' collection, but as a general survey of the relationship between seer-ship, Second Sight, and multifold worlds or dimensions—a survey which he held to contain truth, enduring tradition, and fragments of ancient wisdom."

So was Kirk really taken away by the fairies for writing about second sight and fairylore? Come on, you know we're not going to answer that! There is a grave with Kirk's name on it, but legend has it that there is no body in it (which of course adds to the mystery). The story goes that he was taking a walk, fell, and died . . . but then appeared later to a relative, saying that he was not dead but instead in Fairyland, and that if certain steps were taken at the baptism of his son who was to be soon born, he would be restored to the human world. His friends and family dutifully set everything up, but when a vision of him *did* appear, they were so shocked that they failed to do what they were supposed to do, and Kirk was lost forever.

A Rev. William M. Taylor, quoted by W. Y. Evans-Wentz, said that "at the time of his disappearance, people said he was *taken* because the fairies were displeased with him for prying into their secrets." Those secrets were, of course, the contents of *The Secret Commonwealth*, which is inarguably full of fairylore, though Kirk died (or vanished) before he could publish it himself. Another of Evans-Wentz's informants furnished him with additional infor-mation: "Mrs. J. MacGregor, who keeps the key to the old churchyard where there is a tomb to Kirk, though many say there is nothing in it but a coffin filled with stones, told me that Kirk was taken into the Fairy Knoll, which she pointed to just across a little valley in front of us, and is there yet, for the hill is full of caverns, and in them the 'good people' have their homes. And she added that Kirk appeared to a relative of his after he was taken, and said that he was in the power of the 'good people,' and couldn't get away."

At the very least, the lore places Kirk squarely among the fairies.

# Tam Lin

*Collected by Francis James Child*

## SCOTLAND

To us, "Tam Lin" is one of the greatest fairy stories, and when looking for a tale to include in the "Our Fairies, Ourselves" chapter, we couldn't resist its call. Not only is it a tale of a human spirited away to Fairyland, but it also features a fabulously badass heroine in Janet. Let's face it— she has to be to take on the fairy queen!

O I forbid you, maidens a',
That wear gowd on your hair,
To come or gae by Carterhaugh,
For young Tam Lin is there.

There's nane that gaes by Carterhaugh
But they leave him a wad,
Either their rings, or green mantles,
Or else their maidenhead.

Janet has kilted her green kirtle
A little aboon her knee,
And she has broded her yellow hair
A little aboon her bree,
And she's awa to Carterhaugh
As fast as she can hie.

When she came to Carterhaugh
Tam Lin was at the well,
And there she fand his steed standing,
But away was himsel.

She had na pu'd a double rose,
A rose but only twa,
Till upon then started young Tam Lin,
Says, Lady, thou's pu nae mae.

Why pu's thou the rose, Janet,
And why breaks thou the wand?
Or why comes thou to Carterhaugh
Withoutten my command?

"Carterhaugh, it is my own,
My daddy gave it me,
I'll come and gang by Carterhaugh,
And ask nae leave at thee."

Janet has kilted her green kirtle
A little aboon her knee,
And she has broded her yellow hair
A little aboon her bree,
And she is to her father's ha,
As fast as she can hie.

PART OF THE BALLAD TAM LIN FROM
*COLLECTION OF SCOTTISH FOLK SONGS*
EDITED BY ROBERT BURNS

Four and twenty ladies fair
Were playing at the ba,
And out then came the fair Janet,
The flower among them a'.

Four and twenty ladies fair
Were playing at the chess,
And out then came the fair Janet,
As green as onie glass.

Out then spake an auld grey knight,
Lay oer the castle wa,
And says, Alas, fair Janet, for thee,
But we'll be blamed a'.
"Haud your tongue, ye auld fac'd knight,
Some ill death may ye die!
Father my bairn on whom I will,
I'll father none on thee."

Out then spak her father dear,
And he spak meek and mild,
"And ever alas, sweet Janet," he says,
"I think thou gaest wi child."

"If that I gae wi child, father,
Mysel maun bear the blame,
There's neer a laird about your ha,
Shall get the bairn's name.

"If my love were an earthly knight,
As he's an elfin grey,
I wad na gie my ain true-love
For nae lord that ye hae.

"The steed that my true love rides on
Is lighter than the wind,
Wi siller he is shod before,
Wi burning gowd behind."

Janet has kilted her green kirtle
A little aboon her knee,
And she has broded her yellow hair
A little aboon her bree,
And she's awa to Carterhaugh
As fast as she can hie.

When she came to Carterhaugh,
Tam Lin was at the well,
And there she fand his steed standing,
But away was himsel.

She had na pu'd a double rose,
A rose but only twa,
Till up then started young Tam Lin,
Says, Lady, thou pu's nae mae.

"Why pu's thou the rose, Janet,
Amang the groves sae green,
And a' to kill the bonny babe
That we gat us between?"

"O tell me, tell me, Tam Lin," she says,
"For's sake that died on tree,
If eer ye was in holy chapel,
Or christendom did see?"

"Roxbrugh he was my grandfather,
Took me with him to bide
And ance it fell upon a day
That wae did me betide.

"And ance it fell upon a day
A cauld day and a snell,
When we were frae the hunting come,
That frae my horse I fell,
The Queen o' Fairies she caught me,
In yon green hill do dwell.

"And pleasant is the fairy land,
But, an eerie tale to tell,
Ay at the end of seven years,
We pay a tiend to hell,
I am sae fair and fu o flesh,
I'm feard it be mysel.

"But the night is Halloween, lady,
The morn is Hallowday,
Then win me, win me, an ye will,
For weel I wat ye may.

"Just at the mirk and midnight hour
The fairy folk will ride,
And they that wad their true-love win,
At Miles Cross they maun bide."

"But how shall I thee ken, Tam Lin,
Or how my true-love know,
Amang sa mony unco knights,
The like I never saw?"

"O first let pass the black, lady,
And syne let pass the brown,
But quickly run to the milk-white steed,
Pu ye his rider down.

"For I'll ride on the milk-white steed,
And ay nearest the town,
Because I was an earthly knight
They gie me that renown.

"My right hand will be gloved, lady,
My left hand will be bare,
Cockt up shall my bonnet be,
And kaimed down shall my hair,
And thae's the takens I gie thee,
Nae doubt I will be there.

"They'll turn me in your arms, lady,
Into an esk and adder,
But hold me fast, and fear me not,
I am your bairn's father.

"They'll turn me to a bear sae grim,
And then a lion bold,
But hold me fast, and fear me not,
And ye shall love your child.

"Again they'll turn me in your arms
To a red het gand of airn,
But hold me fast, and fear me not,
I'll do you nae harm.

"And last they'll turn me in your arms
Into the burning gleed,
Then throw me into well water,
O throw me in with speed.

"And then I'll be your ain true-love,
I'll turn a naked knight,
Then cover me wi your green mantle,
And hide me out o sight."

Gloomy, gloomy was the night,
And eerie was the way,
As fair Jenny in her green mantle
To Miles Cross she did gae.

At the mirk and midnight hour
She heard the bridles sing,
She was as glad at that
As any earthly thing.

First she let the black pass by,
And syne she let the brown,
But quickly she ran to the milk-white steed,
And pu'd the rider down.

Sae weel she minded what he did say,
And young Tam Lin did win,
Syne covered him wi her green mantle,
As blythe's a bird in spring
Out then spak the Queen o Fairies,
Out of a bush o broom,
"Them that has gotten young Tam Lin
Has gotten a stately-groom."

Out then spak the Queen o Fairies,
And an angry woman was she,
"Shame betide her ill-far'd face,
And an ill death may she die,
For she's taen awa the bonniest knight
In a' my companie.

"But had I kend, Tam Lin," said she,
"What now this night I see,
I wad hae taen out thy twa grey een,
And put in twa een o tree."

KORPORKUR

JAPAN

# THE RUMORS HAVE BEEN GREATLY EXAGGERATED

The wide variety of fairies we've discussed in this book shows us why we're still so captivated by them hundreds of years after they were supposedly gone from our world forever—they are an endless source of inspiration and a powerful fun-house mirror for humanity. In fact, we would argue that no other creature of folklore can capture the beautiful and terrifying magic of our world and our experiences quite like the fairy does. Angela Bourke writes that fairies were and continue to be "rich sources of inspiration for poets [and other artists largely because they] offer a possibility of expressing things that are generally unspeakable." Through fairies, we can talk about things that are difficult, dangerous, or even impossible to otherwise describe. We use them to express *ourselves*—our fears, our loves, our joys, and our terrors. And that's why they're still here.

As we wrap up our exploration of fairies, we want to conclude by briefly talking about some of the ways that the fairies of folklore have shown up in other media, particularly how they're showing up most often today. After all, fairies are staples of literature, TV, movies, theater, art, fashion, comic books, role-playing games, and so much more!

## THE FAIRIES OF LITERATURE

In our introduction, we mentioned that writers as far back as Chaucer wrote about fairies and, basically, they have never stopped since! In 1590, Edmund Spenser wrote his famous allegory about Queen Elizabeth I using fairies and called it *The Faerie Queene*. Soon after, Shakespeare played a "pivotal role [. . .] in setting forever the limits of what [. . .] English fairies could be and do," as Diane Purkiss writes. There is Mercutio's vivid description of the tiny fairy Queen Mab in *Romeo and Juliet* (1597), the enslaved sprite Ariel in *The Tempest*

(1611), and, of course, the fairies who constitute many of the main characters of the enchanting story of *A Midsummer Night's Dream* (1600). After that, we see stories like Alexander Pope's *The Rape of the Lock* (1712), which contains sylphs and gnomes, and a wealth of literary fairy tales featuring fairies produced in France by aristocratic women.

It was during the late 1700s, however, that Romantics began writing about fairies with a vengeance. Sir Walter Scott, one of the earliest collectors of folklore, wrote "Alice Brand," a fairy ballad inspired by folk ballads, and he included his new creation in his novel *The Lady of the Lake* (1810). Samuel Taylor Coleridge's "Christabel" (1816) is arguably a story about an evil fairy, Percy Bysshe Shelley wrote a poem called "Queen Mab" (1813), and John Keats's "La Belle Dame Sans Merci" (1819) seems to speak of a fairy of seduction. William Blake even wrote of witnessing a fairy funeral himself, with "a procession of creatures of the size and color of green and gray grasshoppers, bearing a body laid out on a rose-leaf, which they buried with songs, and then disappeared," as Katharine Briggs quotes. Over in Germany, Goethe's "Erlkönig" of 1782 is a haunting story about a child who hears the singing of the Erl King, an evil fairy, only to have his father repeatedly dismiss him. As Diane Purkiss observes, when the child dies, it is implied that the father's refusal to acknowledge the reality of the Erl King, "his refusal to know, [is what] dooms his son." The Fairyland of the Romantic period was a strange and frightening and powerful place.

The Victorian period saw many fairy stories, but a lot of them lean decidedly twee (if you want to read something funny, Katharine Briggs on J. M. Barrie's *Peter Pan* [1904] is scathing, largely because she feels he knew better). We do, however, get the masterpiece of "Goblin Market" (1862) from Christina Rossetti, which Purkiss accurately argues "restores fully a sense of the otherness and menace of the fairy world, a sense missing from literary evocations of it since the death of Keats." Other notable contributions of the Victorian age include Robert Browning's "Childe Roland to the Dark Tower Came" (1855), the stunning fairy tales of George MacDonald, and a slew of incredible stage productions that would shape fairy media for long after. Even in the realist work of the period, we can see the influence of fairies—for example, George Eliot's *Silas Marner* (1861) can easily be said to owe a debt to the fairy tale of "Rumpelstiltskin," which, of course, features a fairy as the title character.

In the early twentieth century, writers like Walter de la Mare, Mary de Morgan, Lord Dunsany, and of course W. B. Yeats started bringing fairies back to their more folkloric roots. One of the major and most outspoken proponents of this was actually Rudyard Kipling, whose Puck books drew strongly on older, folkloric ideas of what fairies were supposed to be like. As Briggs writes, "the people who knew what tradition was and were impatient of the airy-fairies on which young intelligences had been fed, began at last to get a hearing" with these kinds of stories. Consider this quotation from Kipling's *Puck of Pook's Hill*, a conversation between the fairy Puck and the human child Dan, published in 1908:

> "Besides, what you call them are made-up things the People of the Hills have never heard of—little buzzflies with butterfly wings and gauze petticoats, and shiny stars in their hair and a wand like a school teacher's cane for punishing bad boys and rewarding good ones! I know 'em!"
>
> "We don't mean that sort," said Dan. "We hate 'em too."
>
> "Exactly," said Puck. "Can you wonder that the People of the Hills don't care to be confused with that painty-winged, wand waving, sugar-and-shake-your-head set of imposters? Butterfly wings indeed!"

Kipling couldn't get much more explicit about his feelings than that!

After that, we move of course to the writings of Oxford's Inklings group, particularly C. S. Lewis's Chronicles of Narnia books (1950-1956), which feature fairylike creatures like satyrs, and J. R. R. Tolkien's *The Hobbit* and *The Lord of the Rings* books (1937, 1954–1955), which we have already mentioned. Katharine Briggs considered Tolkien's books to be the "highwater mark" of "fairy lore in literature," writing that "the distinctive flavor of the elves, dwarves and other creatures is truly preserved without loss of individual characterization" and "to those who yield to the spell of the books they have a compelling atmosphere, and on first reading them no friend is felt to be a companion who is not able to discuss them. It is admission into a world which has objective quality." The complexity and detail of the world of Tolkien's elves is truly unmatched, and we agree that it remains a dazzling example of what fairylore can help a writer achieve.

Contemporary literature remains indebted to fairies, but it's tackling them in new and exciting ways, mixing in postmodern sensibilities and

tactics, a broader appreciation for the subversive potential of fairylore, and an increasing amount of diversity. Writers like Terri Windling, Catherynne M. Valente, Charles de Lint, and Elizabeth Hand are among those doing fascinating work with fairylore today. We also have to mention the recent "sexy fairies" turn in young adult literature. Writers like Holly Black, Melissa Marr, and Sarah J. Maas are at the forefront of this trend. Young adult also seems to be the genre of literature most actively embracing more diverse representations of what fairylore can be—definitely check out the work of Shveta Thakrar, Malinda Lo, Roshani Chokshi, and S. A. Chakraborty. Alexis Hall and Mia Tsai have also written excellent diverse fairy-infused fantasy outside of YA, too! For more traditional but still highly inventive recent takes, we especially recommend *Winter Rose* by Patricia A. McKillip (2002), *Thomas the Rhymer* by Ellen Kushner (2004), and *Jonathan Strange and Mr. Norrell* by Susanna Clarke (2004) (and the TV miniseries it inspired in 2015).

## THE FAIRIES OF FILM AND TELEVISION

Fairies have, of course, also infiltrated film and television. In fact, Skye Alexander points out how much a certain cinematic fairy—Tinkerbell—has even become emblematic of the corporation she represents: "This feisty little pixie, first introduced by J. M. Barrie in his 1904 play *Peter Pan*, made her screen debut in 1953. Since then, the Disney Company has chosen her as its mascot and even given her her own franchise: Disney Fairies. Her image is synonymous with Disney theme parks and she has her own direct-to-DVD film series." In 2010, she even got a star on the Hollywood Walk of Fame, which is pretty wild. Quite impressive for someone who started out as a simple light and a tiny bell on a Victorian stage! Aside from the multiple Disney fairies, from tiny pixies like Tinkerbell to the powerful and majestic Maleficent of their *Sleeping Beauty* (1959) and the later two live-action films devoted to her story (2014 and 2019), fairies do pop up more often in teen and adult video media than you might expect. For example, the television show *Lost Girl* (2010–2016) centered on a succubus named Bo but featured all kinds of fairies and fairylike creatures from folklore. It ran for five seasons, a testament to its popularity. The *Winx Club* animated series (2004–2023), about a group of girls at a fairy school, was recently turned into a live action show, *Fate: The Winx Saga* (2021–2022), which ran for two seasons. In Japan, yōkai are staples in anime, and two

especially striking, folklorically rich examples are CLAMP's *xxxHolic* (2006–2011) and *Mushishi* (2005–2014). There are also, of course, several fairy films that deserve mention, including Jim Henson's *Labyrinth* (1986), Guillermo del Toro's *Pan's Labyrinth* (2006), and *The Spiderwick Chronicles* (2008), which was inspired by a series by Holly Black and recently reimagined as a television show (2024) on Roku as well. There are even a few horror films out there that explicitly draw on fairylore, like *Rawhead Rex* (1986), *Don't Be Afraid of the Dark* (2010), *Unwelcome* (2023), and *The Watchers* (2024).

## FAIRIES BEYOND

We can find fairies in our world in all kinds of other ways, too. They flourish in the beautiful work of contemporary artists like Brian and Wendy Froud, Iris Compiet, Rachel Oakes, Yoshitaka Amano, and Annie Stegg (not to mention the incredible fairy art of centuries past, like that of Arthur Rackham, John Anster Fitzgerald, Edmund Dulac, and even surrealists like Remedios Varo and Leonora Carrington). Music can be inspired by fairylore as well, both in explicit new compositions dedicated to fairies and modern reworkings of fairy ballads. Contemporary musical artists may also draw on fairylore aesthetically if not always explicitly in their work. Florence and the Machine, S. J. Tucker, and Patrick Wolf come to mind as fantastic examples. Fairies also make appearances in video games, from iconic franchises like *Super Mario* and *Legend of Zelda*, to smaller games like *Child of Light* (2014) and *Ori and the Blind Forest* (2015). They're also featured in role-playing games like *Changeling: The Dreaming* (1995), *Changeling: The Lost* (2007), and even *Dungeons & Dragons* (1974–present). Fairy inspirations can even show up in contemporary fashion. Alexander McQueen's gorgeous autumn/winter 2008 collection "The Girl in the Tree" was fairy and fairy-tale themed, and the Museum at the Fashion Institute of Technology in New York City presented an exhibition devoted to fairy-tale fashion in 2016. This exhibition featured countless fabulous, fantastical garments, many of which seemed to be plucked straight out of a fairy legend.

Fairies are still present in our world today even outside artistic media. The Tooth Fairy, for example, remains an extremely popular character to evoke when children lose their baby teeth. Diane Purkiss points out that drawing on a fairy in this situation is actually "quite authentic; she marks

a boundary between one stage of childhood and another. The loss of milk teeth is a drama of growing up and away, a sign that a child is moving out of infancy into middle childhood." Here again we have a fairy presiding over a liminal experience. Frankly, even the Christmas stories of Santa Claus draw heavily on fairy folklore, particularly in their depictions of elves (a fact that the somewhat unsettling Elf on a Shelf toys have certainly exploited).

There are also, we are delighted to say, several festivals that have popped up in recent years specifically to celebrate fairies. These festivals attract artists, musicians, and makers of various kinds, and some of the costumes people wear are simply incredible. They offer a wonderful opportunity to embrace your love of the fair folk, and if you can attend one, we highly recommend doing so.

## THE FUTURE OF FAIRYLORE

So what, then, is the future of fairylore? Well, as folklorists, we're sorry to say that living fairylore can seem pretty thin on the ground in most places. It does still exist on a communal level in some locations—Newfoundland, Ireland, and Iceland, for example—but it's not as widespread or widely embraced as it once was. (Of course, people have been saying this for almost a thousand years at this point, an irony that is not lost on us.) Part of this perceived decline is, we believe, fueled by a rise in stories about aliens, which can mirror, with shocking clarity, fairy abduction stories of earlier times. (Small stature? Temporal confusion? Removal to an unfamiliar realm and a disorienting return? Dancing green lights? We're just saying . . .) And of course, stories about ghosts, which have long been conflated with fairies, are still very much alive.

Fairylore and belief can also be found in some (neo)pagan religions and practices, though they are often very new, recently invented traditions. (That said, Jenny Butler adds that these new religions and belief systems often draw from many different "esoteric knowledge systems, including Theosophy, which is an occult movement that originated in the nineteenth century with roots that can be traced to the ancient philosophical traditions of Gnosticism and Neoplatonism.") Folklorist and historian Simon Young has also made an attempt to reinvigorate the Fairy Investigation Society, an organization that originally ran from 1927 until the early 1990s (and once included Walt

Disney as a member). According to Young, the members of the original organization were required to have a firm belief in the reality of fairies, but his new version is, as their website Fairyist.com puts it, "a secular version of the same; that is to say that it is for all those who have an interest in fairylore, be they believers or ultra skeptics." While this organization has conducted several censuses to attempt to determine the nature of contemporary belief, it is still clear that fairylore has lost many of its true believers . . . or at least it's no longer something many will *admit* to believing in.

As we were finishing this book, a friend told us about a trip she'd taken to Bornholm in Denmark not too long ago. On a tour of the island, she noticed tons of enormous glacial boulders dotting the fields, which she imagined would cause a lot of problems for farmers. When she asked a local about them, the woman told her that every rock was a troll home and that the farmers knew better than to antagonize a troll in their own fields. The woman then asked her to never tell the other Danes in their group what she'd revealed, believing she'd lose face for being superstitious. Still, she thought it was best to leave the boulders alone. If asked directly, this young woman probably would not have said, "Yes, I believe in fairies!" And yet . . .

Again, the fairies are always vanishing but never truly gone: Rumors of the demise of the fairies have been greatly exaggerated! The fairies are still here—they're in our stories and our music and our pop culture. They're in our landscapes, in the trees we won't cut and the rocks we won't move. They're in *us*, when we dress up for a fairy festival or even just put on some sparkling wing earrings to run to the grocery store. Fairies are remarkably resilient . . . and we're pretty sure they're going to be around for a long time yet.

# BIBLIOGRAPHY

Alexander, Skye. *Fairies: The Myths, Legends, and Lore*. Adams Media, 2014.

Andersen, Hans Christian. "The Goblin and the Grocer." In *The Pink Fairy Book*, edited by Andrew Lang, translated by W. A. Craigie, 12–17. Longmans, Green, and Co., 1897.

Angas, George French. *Savage Life and Scenes in Australia and New Zealand*, Vol 1. Smith, Elder and Co., 1847. Reprinted by Libraries Board of South Australia, 1969.

Bacchilega, Cristina, and Marie Alohalani Brown. *The Penguin Book of Mermaids*. Penguin Random House, 2019.

Bane, Theresa. *Encyclopedia of Fairies in World Folklore and Mythology*. McFarland & Company, 2013.

Ben-Amos, Dan. "On Demons." In *Creation and Re-creation in Jewish Thought: Festschrift in Honor of Joseph Dan on the Occasion of His Seventieth Birthday*, 27–38. Mohr Siebeck, 2005.

Birx, H. James, ed. *Encyclopedia of Anthropology*. 5 vols. Sage, 2005.

Bourke, Angela. *The Burning of Bridget Cleary*. Viking, 1999.

Bourke, Angela. "Hunting Out the Fairies: E. F. Benson, Oscar Wilde, and the Burning of Bridget Cleary." In *Wilde the Irishman*, edited by Jerusha McCormack, 36–46. Yale University Press, 1998.

Bourke, Angela. "Reading a Woman's Death: Colonial Text and Oral Tradition in Nineteenth-Century Ireland." *Feminist Studies* 21, no. 3 (1995): 553–586.

Bourke, Angela. "The Virtual Reality of the Irish Fairy Legend." *Éire-Ireland* 31 (1996): 7–25.

Brentano, Clemens Maria. "Lore Lay." 1801. Available at https://allpoetry.com/poem /14371026-Lore-Lay-oder-Zu-Bacharach-am -Rheine-by-Clemens-Maria-Brentano.

Brewster, Adolph B. *The Hill Tribes of Fiji*. Seeley, Service, and Co., 1922.

Briggs, Katharine. *A Dictionary of Fairies: Hobgoblins, Brownies, Bogies, and Other Supernatural Creatures*. Allen Lane, 1976.

Briggs, Katharine. *The Fairies in Tradition and Literature*. Routledge, 1967.

*Britannica*. "Bunyip." *Encyclopedia Britannica*, March 15, 2024. https://www.britannica.com /topic/bunyip.

*Britannica*. "Churning of the ocean of milk." *Encyclopedia Britannica*, March 15, 2024. https://www.britannica.com/topic /churning-of-the-ocean-of-milk.

*Britannica*. "Dybbuk." *Encyclopedia Britannica*, April 10, 2024. https://www.britannica.com /topic/dybbuk-Jewish-folklore.

*Britannica*. "Elf." *Encyclopedia Britannica*, December 28, 2023. https://www.britannica.com/topic /elf-mythology.

*Britannica*. "Garuda." *Encyclopedia Britannica*, November 17, 2023. https://www.britannica.com /topic/Garuda.

*Britannica*. "Ifrit." *Encyclopedia Britannica*, November 28, 2023. https://www.britannica.com /topic/ifrit.

*Britannica*. "Jinni." *Encyclopedia Britannica*, March 27, 2024. https://www.britannica.com /topic/jinni.

*Britannica*. "Leshy." *Encyclopedia Britannica*, October 23, 2023. https://www.britannica.com /topic/leshy.

*Britannica*. "Naga." *Encyclopedia Britannica*, February 23, 2024. https://www.britannica.com/topic/naga-Hindu-mythology.

*Britannica*. "Nix." *Encyclopedia Britannica*, June 19, 2020. https://www.britannica.com/topic/nix-German-mythology.

*Britannica*. "Rakshasa." *Encyclopedia Britannica*, October 27, 2023. https://www.britannica.com/topic/rakshasa.

*Britannica*. "Tengu." *Encyclopedia Britannica*, February 22, 2024. https://www.britannica.com/topic/tengu.

*Britannica*. "Yaksha." *Encyclopedia Britannica*, March 22, 2024. https://www.britannica.com/topic/yaksha.

Bruford, Alan. "Trolls, Hillfolk, Finns, and Picts: The Identity of the Good Neighbors in Orkney and Shetland." In *The Good People: New Fairylore Essays*, edited by Peter Narváez, 116–141. University Press of Kentucky, 1991.

Burns, Robert. "Address to the Devil." 1786. Available at https://www.poetryfoundation.org/poems/43797/address-to-the-devil.

Burton, Adrian. "Who's Afraid of the Curupira?" *Frontiers in Ecology and the Environment* 16, no. 5 (June 2018): 308. https://esajournals.onlinelibrary.wiley.com/doi/full/10.1002/fee.1817.

Butler, Jenny. "The Sídhe and Fairy Forts." In *Magical Folk: British and Irish Fairies 500 AD to the Present*, edited by Simon Young and Ceri Houlbrook, 95–107. Gibson Square, 2018.

Callaway, Henry. *Nursery Tales, Traditions, and Histories of the Zulus*. Trübner and Company, 1868.

Carlson, Marc. "Notes on a Demonic Pantheon." University of Tulsa, February 27, 2012. https://web.archive.org/web/20120227072430/www.personal.utulsa.edu/~marc-carlson/history/demon.txt.

Cashman, Ray. *Packy Jim: Folklore and Worldview on the Irish Border*. University of Wisconsin Press, 2016.

Child, Francis James. *English and Scottish Popular Ballads*. Edited by Helen Child Sargent and George Lyman Kittredge. Houghton Mifflin, 1904.

Child, Francis James. "39A: Tam Lin." In *English and Scottish Popular Ballads*, edited by Helen Child Sargent and George Lyman Kittredge, 66–69. Houghton Mifflin, 1904.

Clarity, James F. "If You Believe in Fairies, Don't Bulldoze Their Lair." *New York Times*, June 16, 1999. https://archive.nytimes.com/www.nytimes.com/learning/teachers/featured_articles/19990616wednesday.html.

Claybourne, Anna. *The Fairy Atlas: Fairy Folk of the World*. Illustrated by Miren Asiain Lora. Laurence King Publishing, 2022.

Craigie, William A. *Scandinavian Folk-Lore: Illustration of the Traditional Belief of the Northern Peoples*. Alexander Gardner, 1896.

Croker, Thomas Crofton. "The Legend of Knockgrafton." In *Fairy and Folk Tales of the Irish Peasantry*, edited by W. B. Yeats, 40–45. Walter Scott, 1888.

Daimler, Morgan. "The Bean Tighe, Invention of an 'Irish' Fairy." Patreon, January 19, 2020. https://www.patreon.com/posts/bean-tighe-of-33284169.

Daimler, Morgan. *A New Dictionary of Fairies: A 21st Century Exploration of Celtic and Related Western European Fairies*. Moon Books, 2020.

Degh, Linda, and Andrew Vazsonyi. "Legend and Belief." In *Folklore Genres*, edited by Dan Ben-Amos, 93–123. University of Texas Press, 1976.

Deshpande, Brahmanand. "Yaksha Worship in Ancient Maharashtra." *Annals of the Bhandarkar Oriental Research Institute* 91 (2010): 91–104.

Dracott, Alice Elizabeth. "The Anar Pari, or The Pomegranate Fairy." In *Simla Village Tales or, Folktales from the Himalayas*, 226–239. John Murray, 1906.

Dracott, Alice Elizabeth. *Simla Village Tales or, Folktales from the Himalayas*. John Murray, 1906.

Eberly, Susan Schoon. "Fairies and the Folklore of Disability: Changelings, Hybrids, and the Solitary Fairy." In *The Good People: New Fairylore Essays*, edited by Peter Narváez, 227–250. University Press of Kentucky, 1991.

Evans-Wentz, W. Y. *The Fairy-Faith in Celtic Countries*. Henry Frowde, 1911; Lost Library, 2016.

Faries, Jordan. "The Mischievous Muki." *CIM Magazine*, September 21, 2018. https://magazine.cim.org/en/in-search/the-mischievous-muki-en.

Fatha, N., M. Adam, R. A. Manaku, and S. Tangkilisan. "Cultural Appropriation of Polynesian Portrayed in *Moana* Movie." *Notion: Journal of Linguistics, Literature, and Culture* 3, no. 2 (2021): 92–98.

Fordred-Green, Lesley. "Tokoloshe Tales: Reflections on the Cultural Politics of Journalism in South Africa." *Current Anthropology* 41, no. 5 (2000): 701–712.

Foster, Michael Dylan. *The Book of Yōkai: Mysterious Creatures of Japanese Folklore*. University of California Press, 2015.

Furr, Josh. "Haunting Ladies of Japan: A Glimpse into the Terrifying World of Female Yōkai." Your Japan, October 31, 2023. https://itsyourjapan.com/haunting-ladies-of-japan-a-glimpse-into-the-terrifying-world-of-female-yokai.

Géo de Siqueira, Maria Fantinato. "'We Are Losing Our Encantados Because We Can't Hear Them Anymore': Silence, Extractivism, and Politics of Listening in/to the Brazilian Amazon." *World of Music* 10, no. 2 (2021): 21–50.

Geoffrey of Monmouth. "La Vita Merlini." Translated by John Jay Parry. 1925. Available at Internet Sacred Texts Archive, https://sacred-texts.com/neu/eng/vm/vmlat.htm.

Goldstücker, Theodor. *A Dictionary, Sanskrit and English*. Philip Pereira, 1856.

Gruber, Anya. "The Modern Resurrection of the Dybbuk, Demon of Jewish Folklore: How a Superstition Goes from the Talmud to TikTok." Atlas Obscura, October 10, 2023. https://www.atlasobscura.com/articles/dybbuk-demon-of-jewish-folklore.

Gunnell, Terry. "Introduction." In *Hildur, Queen of the Elves*, by Jane M. Bedell, 11. Interlink Books, 2007.

Hadler, Jeffrey. *Muslims and Matriarchs: Cultural Resilience in Indonesia Through Jihad and Colonialism*. Cornell University Press, 2008.

Hearn, Lafcadio. "Story of a Tengu." In *In Ghostly Japan*, 215–221. Little, Brown and Company, 1919.

Heine, Heinrich. "The Lorelei." Translated by Anna Leader. 1824. Available at https://classicalpoets.org/2020/01/the-lorelei-by-heinrich-heine/.

Henderson, William. *Folklore of the Northern Counties of England and the Borders*, 2nd ed. W. Satchell, Peyton & Co., 1879.

Hillard, Molly Clark. *Spellbound: The Fairy Tale and the Victorians*. Ohio State University Press, 2014.

Holm, David. "The Exemplar of Filial Piety and the End of the Ape-Men Dong Yong in Guangxi and Guizhou Ritual Performance." *T'oung Pao* 90, no. 1/3 (2004): 32–64.

Houlbrook, Ceri. "The Seelie and Unseelie Courts." In *Magical Folk: British and Irish Fairies 500 AD*

*to the Present*, edited by Simon Young and Ceri Houlbrook, 108-122. Gibson Square, 2018.

Hutton, Ronald. *Witches, Druids, and King Arthur*. Hambledon & London, 2006.

Idema, Wilt L. *The Metamorphosis of Tianxian Pei: Local Opera Under the Revolution (1949-1956)*. Chinese University Press, 2015.

"Indigenous Australians: Australia's First Peoples Exhibition 1996-2015." Australian Museum. https://australian.museum/about/history /exhibitions/indigenous-australians. Accessed October 9, 2024.

Keightley, Thomas. *The Fairy Mythology*. George Bell and Sons, 1892.

Kendall, Laurel. "Wood Imps, Ghosts, and Other Noxious Influences: The Ideology of Affliction in a Korean Village." *Journal of Korean Studies* 3 (1981): 113-145.

Kennedy, Patrick. *Legendary Fictions of the Irish Celts*. Macmillan and Co., 1866.

Kincaid, C. A. *Folk Tales of Sind and Gujarat*. Daily Gazette Press, 1925.

King, Rachel. "Cattle, Raiding and Disorder in Southern African History." *Africa: Journal of the International African Institute* 87, no. 3 (2017): 607-630.

Kipling, Rudyard. *Puck of Pook's Hill*. Bernhard Tauchnitz, 1906.

Knappert, Jan. *African Mythology: An Encyclopedia of Myth and Legend*. Diamond Books, 1995.

Kononenko, Natalie. *Slavic Folklore: A Handbook*. Greenwood Press, 2007.

Krige, Eileen Jensen. *The Social System of the Zulus*. Longmans, Green, and Co., 1936.

Landry, Timothy R. Personal communication, email message to the authors, October 11, 2024.

Lang, Andrew. "Fairy." In *Encyclopædia Britannica*, 11th ed., edited by Hugh Chisholm, vol. 10, 134-135. University of Cambridge, 1911.

Lang, Andrew. "The History of the Book and Author." In *The Secret Commonwealth of Elves, Fauns, and Fairies*, by Robert Kirk, 13-42. Dover, 2008.

Lang, Andrew. *The Pink Fairy Book*. Longmans, Green, and Co., 1897.

Lysaght, Patricia. *The Banshee: The Irish Death Messenger*. Glendale Press, 1986.

MacKillip, James. *Dictionary of Celtic Mythology*. Oxford University Press, 1998.

Magel, Emil Anthony. *Folktales from the Gambia: Wolof Fictional Narratives*. Three Continents Press, 1984.

Malory, Thomas. *King Arthur and His Knights*, edited by Eugene Vinaver. Oxford University Press, 1975.

Martinez, Napoleon. "The Curse of the Nuno Sa Punso." USC Digital Folklore Archives, University of Southern California, April 30, 2017. https:// folklore.usc.edu/the-curse-of-the-nuno-sa-punso.

Martins, Kim. "Menehune." *World History Encyclopedia*. World History Publishing, August 29, 2022. https://www.worldhistory .org/Menehune.

Marzolph, Ulrich. "The Middle Eastern World's Contribution to Fairy-Tale History." In *The Fairy Tale World*, edited by Andrew Teverson, 46, 52, 53. Routledge, 2019.

Metcalfe, M. "Some Nyasaland Folk-Lore Tales." *Nyasaland Journal* 7, no. 2 (1954): 46-49.

Miller, Laura Marjorie. "Sea Lion Woman: A Selkie Story for a New Millennium." *Seven Miles of Steel Thistles*, January 24, 2014. https://steelthistles .blogspot.com/2014/01/sea-lion-woman-selkie -story-for-new.html.

Millington, W. H., and Berton L. Maxfield. "Philippine (Visayan) Superstitions." *Journal of American Folklore* 19, no. 74 (1906): 205-211.

Mulvaney, Amy. "Double Take: The Fairy Bush in Co Clare That Moved a Motorway." *The Journal*, April 24, 2019. https://www.thejournal.ie /fairy-bush-co-clare-4604485-Apr20194.

Munro, Joyce Underwood. "The Invisible Made Visible: The Fairy Changeling as a Folk Articulation of Failure to Thrive in Infants and Children." In *The Good People: New Fairylore Essays*, edited by Peter Narváez, 251–283. University Press of Kentucky, 1991.

Nakamura, Kyoko Motomochi, trans. *Miraculous Stories from the Japanese Buddhist Tradition: The Nihon Ryoiki of the Monk Kyokai.* Harvard University Press, 1973.

Narváez, Peter. "Introduction." In *The Good People: New Fairylore Essays*, edited by Peter Narváez, ix–xiv. University Press of Kentucky, 1991.

Narváez, Peter. "Newfoundland Berry Pickers 'In the Fairies': Maintaining Spatial, Temporal, and Moral Boundaries Through Legendry." In *The Good People: New Fairylore Essays*, edited by Peter Narváez, 336–368. University Press of Kentucky, 1991.

Niehaus, Isak. "Witches of the Transvaal Lowveld and Their Familiars: Conceptions of Duality, Power, and Desire." *Cahiers d'Études Africaines* 35, no. 138/139 (1995): 513–540.

Nizami. *The Haft Paikar.* Translated by C. E. Wilson. Stephen Austin and Sons, Limited, 1914.

O'Connor, Maureen. "The Picture of Dorian Gray as Irish National Tale." In *Writing Irishness in Nineteenth-Century British Culture*, edited by Neil McCaw, 194–209. Ashgate, 2004.

Ó Giolláin, Diarmuid. "The Leipreachán and Fairies, Dwarfs and the Household Familiar: A Comparative Study." *Béaloideas* 52 (1984): 75–150.

Ó hÓgáin, Dáithí. *Irish Superstitions: Irish Spells, Old Wives Tales and Folk Beliefs.* Gill Books, 2002.

*Oxford English Dictionary*. "Fairy, n. and adj." March 2018. www.oed.com/view/Entry/67741.

Piggott, Stuart. *The Druids.* Thames and Hudson, 1968.

Politz, Sarah. *Transforming Vòdún: Musical Change and Postcolonial Healing in Benin's Jazz and Brass Band Music.* University of Michigan Press, 2023.

Pu, Songling. *Strange Tales from a Chinese Studio.* Edited and translated by John Minford. Penguin Books, 2006.

Purkiss, Diane. *At the Bottom of the Garden: A Dark History of Fairies, Hobgoblins, and Other Troublesome Things.* New York University Press, 2003.

Ralston, W. R. S. *The Songs of the Russian People: As Illustrative of Slavonic Mythology and Russian Social Life.* Ellis and Green, 1872.

*The Ramayana.* Translated by Arshia Sattar. Penguin, 2003.

*The Ramayana.* Translated by Ralph T. H. Griffith. Trübner & Co, 1870–1874. Available at Project Gutenberg. https://www.gutenberg.org/files /24869/24869-h/24869-h.html.

Rieti, Barbara. *Strange Terrain: The Fairy World in Newfoundland.* Institute of Social and Economic Research, Memorial University of Newfoundland, 1991.

Rink, Hinrich (Henry). *Tales and Traditions of the Eskimo: With a Sketch of Their Habits, Religion, Language and Other Peculiarities.* William Blackwood and Sons, 1875.

Rodríguez-Mejía, Fredy, and James D. Sexton, eds. *The Dog Who Spoke and More Mayan Folktales: El Perro Que Habló y Más Cuentos Mayas.* University of Oklahoma Press, 2014.

Rojcewicz, Peter M. "Between One Eye Blink and the Next: Fairies, UFOs, and Problems of Knowledge." In *The Good People: New Fairylore Essays*, edited by Peter Narváez, 479–514. University Press of Kentucky, 1991.

Schacker, Jennifer. *Staging Fairyland: Folklore, Children's Entertainment, and Nineteenth-Century Pantomime.* Wayne State University Press, 2018.

Sharpe, Victoria. "The Goddess Restored." *Journal of the Fantastic in the Arts* 9, no. 1 (1998): 36–45.

Sibley, Barbara Jean. "The Prince-Charming Syndrome: Case History of an Imaginary Suitor." *Philippine Sociological Review* 18, no. 2 (1970): 93–97.

Sikes, Wirt. *British Goblins: Welsh Folk-lore, Fairy Mythology, Legends, and Traditions.* Sampson Low, 1880. Republished by the Lost Library, 2010.

Silver, Carole G. *Strange and Secret Peoples: Fairies and Victorian Consciousness.* Oxford University Press, 1999.

Somadeva. *Tales from the Kathasaritasagara.* Edited and translated by Arshia Sattar. Penguin Books, 1994.

Spence, Lewis. "The Lorelei." In *Hero Tales and Legends of the Rhine*, 59–61. George C. Harrap and Company, 1915.

Spivack, Charlotte. "Morgan Le Fay: Goddess or Witch?" In *Popular Arthurian Traditions*, edited by Sally K. Slocum, 18–23. Bowling Green State University Popular Press, 1992.

Stewart, R. J. *Robert Kirk: Walker Between the Worlds: A New Edition of* The Secret Commonwealth of Elves, Fauns, and Fairies. R. J. Stewart Books, 2007.

Sugg, Richard. "Fairy Magic and the Cottingley Photographs." In *Magical Folk: British and Irish Fairies 500 AD to the Present*, edited by Simon Young and Ceri Houlbrook, 54–64. Gibson Square, 2018.

Todhunter, J. "How Thomas Connolly Met the Banshee." In *Fairy and Folk Tales of the Irish Peasantry*, edited by W.B. Yeats, 109–112. Walter Scott, 1888.

Thoms, William. *Lays and Legends of Various Nations: Lays and Legends of France.* George Cowie, 1834.

Tomlinson, Matt. "Little People, Ghosts, and the Anthropology of the Good." *Journal of the Polynesian Society* 125, no. 1 (2016): 11–32.

Tregear, E. R. *Maori-Polynesian Comparative Dictionary.* Christchurch: Lyon and Blair, 1891.

Warman, Brittany. *The Fae, the Fairy Tale, and the Gothic Aesthetic in Nineteenth-Century British Literature.* PhD diss., Ohio State University, 2018.

Werner, A. "Abatwa Tradition." *Man* 15 (1915): 72–73.

Wilde, Jane. *Ancient Legends, Mystic Charms, and Superstitions of Ireland with Sketches of the Irish Past.* 1888. Reprint, Chatto and Windus, 1925.

Wilson, Monica Hunter. "Witch Beliefs and Social Structure." *American Journal of Sociology* 56, no. 4 (1951): 307–313.

Witthoft, John, and Wendell S. Hadlock. "Cherokee-Iroquois Little People." *Journal of American Folklore* 59, no. 234 (1946): 413–422.

Wood, Juliette. "Celtic Goddesses: Myths and Mythology." In *The Feminist Companion to Mythology*, edited by Carolyne Larrington, 118–136. Pandora Press, 1992.

Wrede, Patricia C. "The Lorelai." In *The Book of Enchantments.* Clarion Books, 2005.

Yaganita, Kunio. *The Legends of Tono: 100th Anniversary Editions.* Translated by Ronald A. Morse. Lexington Books, 2008.

Yeats, W. B., ed. *Fairy and Folk Tales of the Irish Peasantry.* Walter Scott, 1888.

Young, Simon. *Fairyist.* Fairy Investigation Society, 2013. https://www.fairyist.com. Accessed October 6, 2024.

Young, Simon. "A History of the Fairy Investigation Society, 1927–1960." *Folklore* 124, no. 2 (2013): 139–156.

Zipes, Jack. "Witch and Fairy / Fairy as Witch: Unfathomable Baba Yagas." In *The Irresistible Fairy Tale: The Cultural and Social History of a Genre*, 55–79. Princeton University Press, 2013.

# NOTES

## INTRODUCTION: FAIRIES BETWEEN HEAVEN AND HELL

14 *From the beginning*: We'd also like to acknowledge upfront that the word "fairy" was used for a significant period of time as a slur against homosexual men. The first official use in print of the word "fairy" to mean "an effeminate or homosexual man" was, according to the Oxford English Dictionary, in 1895 in the US. As Angela Bourke points out, however, it makes sense to suspect people were using the word that way long before it appeared anywhere in print (Bourke, "Hunting Out the Fairies").

15 *generalized, sometimes overlapping words*: We've largely steered clear of the word "dwarf" in this collection because it comes with an absolutely massive amount of complicated baggage. While dwarfs (the plural "dwarves" was actually made up by Tolkien!) proliferate in folklore and fantasy literature, there are also real people with a medical condition called dwarfism, and many depictions of magical dwarfs flirt with (or topple headlong) into antisemitic tropes. For these reasons, and because there's almost always another, more precise word to use instead, we're choosing to use other terminology here.

15 *the English word "elf"*: Folklorist Alan Bruford argues the form more likely came to English through Scots, as it was a more usual term than "fairy" when the northern islands there were being colonized from Scotland. There is even some documentation that suggests "elf" was used to refer to a male fairy while "fairy" meant a female fairy! That said, it's very likely that *those* islands did originally get "elf" from the Old Norse word (Bruford, "Trolls, Hillfolk, Finns, and Picts").

16 *"Fairy . . . is the common term"*: Lang, "Fairy."

17 *it was very possible for tales to spread*: Purkiss, *At the Bottom of the Garden*.

18 *medieval magicians calling upon sylphs*: Silver, *Strange and Secret Peoples*. Silver notes that Anna Kingsford and Herbert Arnold rejected conflating fairies with elementals early on, arguing that each kind of being was distinctly different, but we maintain that there is significant overlap (at least enough to mix the two in popular imagination).

18 *"personifications of disruptive forces of nature"*: Silver, *Strange and Secret Peoples*.

18 *this connection only occurs "sometimes"*: Purkiss, *At the Bottom of the Garden*.

19 *"red suits, [to] flowing gowns"*: Narváez, "Introduction."

19 *"protean beings"*: Rieti, *Strange Terrain*.

19 *"as a rule, [they] are described in legend"*: Evans-Wentz, *The Fairy-Faith in Celtic Countries*.

19 *An anonymous Irish mystic*: Evans-Wentz, *The Fairy-Faith in Celtic Countries*.

21 *"The Legend of Knockgrafton"*: Croker, "The Legend of Knockgrafton." This was originally published in his collection *Fairy Legends and Traditions of the South of Ireland* (John Murray, 1825).

21 *Irish fairy music is beautiful but limited*: Warman, *The Fae, the Fairy Tale, and the Gothic Aesthetic*.

22 *"the distinction between the fairies and the dead"*: Briggs, *The Fairies in Tradition and Literature*.

22 *"the connection between fairies and prehistoric burial mounds"*: Butler, "The Sídhe and Fairy Forts."

22 *"there has long been in Irish folklore"*: Cashman, *Packy Jim*.

22 *"those killed before their time"*: Briggs, *The Fairies in Tradition and Literature*. Yes, really.

22 *"the greatest number of believers"*: Briggs, *The Fairies in Tradition and Literature*.

23 *"The idea of the fairies as fallen or neutral angels"*: Cashman, *Packy Jim*.

24 *"all psychic experiences were deeply suspect"*: Briggs, *The Fairies in Tradition and Literature*.

24 *much more common for Christian people*: Briggs, *The Fairies in Tradition and Literature*.

25 *"fusion and confusion"*: Zipes, "Witch and Fairy / Fairy as Witch."

25 *God was visiting the earth*: Briggs, *The Fairies in Tradition and Literature*.

26 *Evans-Wentz considered it*: Evans-Wentz, *The Fairy-Faith in Celtic Countries*.

26 *and, as Diane Purkiss notes*: Purkiss, *At the Bottom of the Garden*.

26 *"people of the goddess Danu"*: Or Anú.

26 *"The Tuatha Dé Danann became associated"*: Butler, "The Sídhe and Fairy Forts."

27 *"nymphs [etc.] are caught between"*: Purkiss, *At the Bottom of the Garden*.

28 *"the Pygmy Theory"*: Evans-Wentz, *The Fairy-Faith in Celtic Countries*. Note that the word "pygmy" is no longer used and is now considered derogatory.

28 *"This race is supposed to have"*: Evans-Wentz, *The Fairy-Faith in Celtic Countries*.

28 *This is supposed to*: Purkiss, *At the Bottom of the Garden*.

28 *it allows fairies to be real*: Purkiss, *At the Bottom of the Garden*.

29 *"past-as-wished-for"*: Piggot, *The Druids*.

29 *the few written sources*: Wood, "Celtic Goddesses."

29 *"In their hands"*: Purkiss, *At the Bottom of the Garden*. From *Romeo and Juliet* (1597).

30 *"birth, childhood, and its transitions"*: Purkiss, *At the Bottom of the Garden*.

30 *"The heaven-world of the ancient Celts"*: Evans-Wentz, *The Fairy-Faith in Celtic Countries*.

30 *The Naga, a half-human, half-snake*: Britannica, "Naga."

31 *And in the Cook Islands*: Claybourne, *The Fairy Atlas*.

31 *W. B. Yeats divided*: Yeats, *Fairy and Folk Tales of the Irish Peasantry*.

31 *"We were told as children"*: Evans-Wentz, *The Fairy-Faith in Celtic Countries.*

33 *"power as disruptive forces"*: Silver, *Strange and Secret Peoples.*

33 *Scottish fairies that "appeared to be aristocratic"*: Houlbrook, "The Seelie and Unseelie Courts."

33 *"legends describe the Seelie"*: Alexander 2014.

33 *fairies "are great lovers of cleanliness"*: Briggs, *The Fairies in Tradition and Literature.*

33 *"Sometimes a year is really"*: Briggs, *The Fairies in Tradition and Literature.*

35 *They are stories with a "truth status"*: Degh and Vazsonyi, "Legend and Belief."

38 *fairies "demand appropriate responses"*: Narváez, "Introduction."

38 *parts of the "changeling tradition"*: Narváez, "Introduction."

38 *By saying "No, no"*: Narváez, "Introduction."

38 *used as "alibis"*: As recently as 1895, an Irish man named Michael Cleary (alongside several other members of his community) murdered his wife, Bridget Cleary, by setting her on fire because he claimed she was a fairy changeling. They all said they believed that Cleary's real wife had been stolen by the fairies, that a changeling creature had been left in her place, and that the changeling was the one they burned. Cleary firmly believed (or at least said he firmly believed) that his true wife would come back, riding a white horse, once the changeling was destroyed. If you'd like to read more about this story, we highly recommend Angela Bourke's excellent (but horrifying) book *The Burning of Bridget Cleary* and her original article on the subject, "Reading a Woman's Death."

38 *"functioned as agents of social control"*: Narváez, "Introduction."

39 *Many of us are not embedded*: We're talking since the time of Shakespeare at least, but probably even before that.

40 *Sure, sometimes a fairy will*: No lie. See the "Dullahan" in our "Fairies of Terror" chapter.

41 *"This book is an imperfect . . . creature"*: Purkiss, *At the Bottom of the Garden.*

42 *From as far back as Chaucer*: This is from the beginning of the "Wife of Bath's Tale" in his book *The Canterbury Tales* (1392).

42 *they "have never quite left"*: Silver, *Strange and Secret Peoples.*

42 *"Rare, tenuous and fragile as it is"*: Briggs, *The Fairies in Tradition and Literature.*

## CHAPTER 1: FAIRIES OF THE HOME

48 *"industrious and helpful household spirit"*: Briggs, *The Fairies in Tradition and Literature.*

48 *"small, wizened and shaggy"*: Briggs, *The Fairies in Tradition and Literature.*

48 *"generally grotesque to look at"*: Briggs, *The Fairies in Tradition and Literature.*

48 *"so expert in hiding"*: Briggs, *The Fairies in Tradition and Literature.*

48 *"sweeping, churning, spinning"*: Briggs, *The Fairies in Tradition and Literature.*

48 *"fetching the midwife"*: Briggs, *The Fairies in Tradition and Literature.*

48 *"A Brownie on the Celtic fringe"*: Briggs, *The Fairies in Tradition and Literature.*

51 *The name "zashiki-warashi" translates as*: Foster, *The Book of Yōkai.*

51 *"The mother of Kizen Sasaski"*: As quoted in Foster, *The Book of Yōkai.*

51 *He has a connection to changeling lore*: Foster, *The Book of Yōkai.*

52 *"He acts as the intermediary"*: Kononenko, *Slavic Folklore.*

53 *"direct invocation"*: Briggs, *The Fairies in Tradition and Literature.*

53 *"a grotesque creature"*: Briggs, *The Fairies in Tradition and Literature.*

53 *"play other tricks too"*: Claybourne, *The Fairy Atlas.*

55 *More specifically, "The Alux"*: Birx, *Encyclopedia of Anthropology.*

55 *called duendecillo*: Birx, *Encyclopedia of Anthropology.*

55 *"serves a social function"*: Birx, *Encyclopedia of Anthropology.*

55 *"it cannot be ascertained"*: Rodríguez-Mejía and Sexton, *The Dog Who Spoke.*

56 *try to infiltrate a house*: Claybourne, *The Fairy Atlas.*

56 *Laurel Kendall explains*: Kendall, "Wood Imps, Ghosts, and Other Noxious Influences."

56 *"'My mother-in-law was sick'"*: Kendall, "Wood Imps, Ghosts, and Other Noxious Influences."

57 *"A Cho man suffered"*: Kendall, "Wood Imps, Ghosts, and Other Noxious Influences."

58 *"the old custom is to leave food"*: Claybourne, *The Fairy Atlas.*

59 *"the form of a boy doll"*: Rodríguez-Mejía and Sexton, *The Dog Who Spoke.*

59 *"they hide in the walls"*: Claybourne, *The Fairy Atlas.*

59 *both Hispanic and Mayan*: Rodríguez-Mejía and Sexton, *The Dog Who Spoke.*

59 *"knocking and banging"*: Claybourne, *The Fairy Atlas.*

59 *"either there is a hidden treasure"*: Claybourne, *The Fairy Atlas.*

60 *Should "you manage to snatch"*: Claybourne, *The Fairy Atlas.*

60 *You can evade him*: Incidentally, these are both time-honored tactics for dealing with vampires, too.

61 *"When purchasing a new farm animal"*: Kononenko, *Slavic Folklore.*

63 *They're child-sized*: Ó Giolláin, "The Leipreachán and Fairies."

63 *"behaves like a poltergeist"*: Ó Giolláin, "The Leipreachán and Fairies."

64 *especially delighted by moonlight*: Keightley, *The Fairy Mythology.*

65 *The grocer ensures*: Andersen, "The Goblin and the Grocer."

66 *"the fairy housekeeper"*: Evans-Wentz, *The Fairy-Faith in Celtic Countries.*

66 *"bean-tighe" literally just means*: Daimler, "The Bean Tighe."

66 *"It seems clear that the passage"*: Daimler, "The Bean Tighe."

69 *"The Goblin and the Grocer"*: Andersen, "The Goblin and the Grocer."

76   *Though she doesn't usually*: We say "usually" because Carole G. Silver does describe a story by early Irish folklorist William Carleton that describes a Lianhan Shee (the term he uses) "who, like a leech, fastened onto a woman, appearing as a protuberance behind her neck" and tormented her (Silver, *Strange and Secret Peoples*). That certainly sounds like actual bloodsucking to us, though this is the only story we know that describes this fairy quite like this!

77   *"The Leanhaun Shee (fairy mistress)"*: Yeats, *Fairy and Folk Tales of the Irish Peasantry*.

77   *"the Leanan-Sidhe, or the spirit of life"*: Wilde, *Ancient Legends*.

78   *a vila was said to have befriended*: Kononenko, *Slavic Folklore*.

81   *"these shapeshifting, irresistibly beautiful"*: Minford in Pu, *Strange Tales from a Chinese Studio*.

81   *They're very seductive*: Minford in Pu, *Strange Tales from a Chinese Studio*.

81   *The hulijing were attractive but dangerous*: Minford in Pu, *Strange Tales from a Chinese Studio*.

82   *According to folklorist Michael Dylan Foster*: Foster, *The Book of Yōkai*.

83   *"overlap and mutually influence"*: Foster, *The Book of Yōkai*.

84   *it might seem like the most seductive fairies*: That said, Carole G. Silver does rightly note that it was "*folklorists* who chose what to collect and emphasize" in this regard, and, frankly, "it seems fairly evident that male preoccupation with female control contributed to the retelling of so many tales of deadly supernatural women" and "equally evident that these tales often expressed anxiety about what might happen if men did not separate and domesticate female power and female sexuality" (Silver, *Strange and Secret Peoples*). Sing it, Carole.

84   *"handsome with pale, glowing skin"*: Claybourne, *The Fairy Atlas*. If you're getting Edward Cullen vibes here, we wouldn't blame you.

84   *Barbara Jean Sibley describes*: Sibley, "The Prince-Charming Syndrome."

85   *They can try the kidnapping move*: Millington and Maxfield, "Philippine (Visayan) Superstitions."

86   *They married and had three daughters*: Thoms, *Lays and Legends of Various Nations*.

87   *"Then as the waters foamed and boiled"*: *Ramayana* (Griffith translation).

88   *"Nikusui is a femme-fatal"*: Furr, "Haunting Ladies of Japan."

89   *gwragedd annwn "are the nearest thing"*: Briggs, *The Fairies in Tradition and Literature*.

89   *Almost always, the man*: In folkloric terms, this is called "the violation of the interdiction."

90   *"the Morgan is a fairy eternally young"*: Evans-Wentz, *The Fairy-Faith in Celtic Countries*.

91   *"enticing young human men"*: Claybourne, *The Fairy Atlas*.

92   *"Lord Bishop, let me die!"*: Brentano 1801, "Lore Lay."

93   *"The loveliest young maiden sits"*: Heine 1824, "The Lorelei."

95   *"[A] rusalka typically sits in a tree"*: Kononenko, *Slavic Folklore*.

95   *"rusalki were said to tickle"*: Kononenko, *Slavic Folklore*.

96   *"The Lorelei"*: Spence, "The Lorelei."

# CHAPTER 3: FAIRIES OF TERROR

102   *The horns are probably*: Foster, *The Book of Yōkai.*

102   *"a nasty otherworldly being"*: Foster, *The Book of Yōkai.*

102   *And they're recognizable there*: Foster, *The Book of Yōkai.*

104   *"The Good Woman"*: Croker, "The Legend of Knockgrafton."

104   *Other legends say that if you are foolish enough*: Croker, "The Legend of Knockgrafton."

104   *"It was strange music"*: Croker, "The Legend of Knockgrafton."

105   *"the word Dulachan"*: Croker, "The Legend of Knockgrafton."

106   *"a great high black coach"*: Croker, "The Legend of Knockgrafton."

107   *"towers where dark deeds had been done"*: Briggs, *The Fairies in Tradition and Literature.*

108   *They carry little bells*: In this part of the world, bells appear in many cultural situations where liminality, the supernatural, death, and respect overlap. Our colleague Misty L. Bastian told us that, among her Igbo-speaking informants, bells are rung when dangerous figures, like the sacred, not-quite-dead, not-quite-alive Onitsha king, come walking through the town. This way, you know to respectfully avoid them. Bells might also be rung by those walking behind a corpse or by dancers who wear bells on their ankles and wrists as they perform significant dances.

108   *"One day a hunter took his wife"*: Knappert, *African Mythology.*

109   *This is essentially a cautionary tale*: Our thanks to Misty L. Bastion for her insight on this fairy.

110   *Or maybe she's a descendent*: Lysaght, *The Banshee*; MacKillip, *Dictionary of Celtic Mythology*; Daimler, *A New Dictionary of Fairies.*

110   *Sometimes, long tongs are used*: Ó hÓgáin, *Irish Superstitions.*

110   *"Sometimes the Banshee assumes the form"*: Quoted in Briggs, *The Fairies in Tradition and Literature.*

112   *"they have large heads with big, black eyes"*: Claybourne, *The Fairy Atlas.*

112   *They mostly eat bananas and milk*: Claybourne, *The Fairy Atlas.*

113   *It's considered very bad luck*: Claybourne, *The Fairy Atlas.*

113   *Stories about these spirits*: Britannica, "Dybbuk."

113   *A few recent horror movies*: Gruber, "The Modern Resurrection of the Dybbuk."

114   *"recite their magic spells aloud"*: Claybourne, *The Fairy Atlas.* Metal AF.

115   *They make their home in limestone caves*: Claybourne, *The Fairy Atlas.*

115   *A noted deev pastime*: Claybourne, *The Fairy Atlas.*

116   *Rákshasas are 'malevolent'*: Ramayana (Sattar translation).

116   *They can shapeshift at will*: Britannica, "Rakshasa."

116   *"The brave Vijayadatta"*: Ramayana (Sattar translation).

119   *the bunyip as a gigantic starfish*: Angas, *Savage Life and Scenes in Australia and New Zealand*, p. 99.

121   *Michael Dylan Foster, a folklorist specializing*: Foster, *The Book of Yōkai.*

121 *"In Heian-period texts"*: Briggs, *The Fairies in Tradition and Literature.*

123 *"One story commonly told"*: Briggs, *The Fairies in Tradition and Literature.*

124 *"When thowes dissolve the snawy hoord"*: Burns, "Address to the Devil."

124 *Kelpies are . . . far from the only*: See our sidebar on the nix on page 122.

126 *They can be understood as*: Britannica, "Jinni."

126 *"from mouth to foot had her existence"*: Nizami, *The Haft Paikar.*

127 *"inhabiting the earth but unseen"*: Britannica, "Jinni."

127 *They "are beings of smokeless flame"*: Britannica, "Jinni."

127 *"jinn are capable of assuming"*: Britannica, "Jinni."

128 *"the image or trope of the tikoloshe"*: King, "Cattle, Raiding and Disorder."

128 *the tikoloshe familiar "is of opposite sex"*: Wilson, "Witch Beliefs and Social Structure."

128 *a source that claims the tikoloshe's penis*: Niehaus, "Witches of the Transvaal Lowveld."

129 *the "tokolose symbolizes illicit sexual desires"*: Niehaus, "Witches of the Transvaal Lowveld."

129 *Despite this seeming usefulness*: Niehaus, "Witches of the Transvaal Lowveld."

130 *In a pinch, bow to a kappa*: Foster, *The Book of Yōkai.*

130 *"numerous local rituals and festivals"*: Foster, *The Book of Yōkai.*

131 *Many of these names refer to an animal*: Foster, *The Book of Yōkai.*

131 *"This slimy creature"*: Foster, *The Book of Yōkai.*

132 *"essence of the home"*: Kononenko, *Slavic Folklore.*

132 *"Supposedly, the proper thing to do"*: Kononenko, *Slavic Folklore.*

133 *"How Thomas Connolly Met the Banshee"*: Todhunter, "How Thomas Connolly Met the Banshee."

## CHAPTER 4: FAIRIES OF NATURE

140 *When spring does finally defeat her*: Briggs, *A Dictionary of Fairies.*

140 *a remnant of a lost mythical figure*: Briggs, *A Dictionary of Fairies.*

141 *the curupira will punish you*: Claybourne, *The Fairy Atlas.*

141 *a garden in the Amazon as well*: Burton, "Who's Afraid of the Curupira?"

141 *a specific kind of ant is responsible*: Burton, "Who's Afraid of the Curupira?"

143 *Peris are "delicate, winged creatures"*: Claybourne, *The Fairy Atlas.*

143 *They're usually depicted*: Marzolph 2019.

143 *They don't eat food*: Claybourne, *The Fairy Atlas.*

143 *These stories often feature broken taboos*: Marzolph, "The Middle Eastern World's Contribution."

144 *They live in the forest*: Claybourne, *The Fairy Atlas.*

144 *"large fuzzy mops of hair"*: Brewster, *The Hill Tribes of Fiji.*

144 *"decidedly contrary"*: Tomlinson, "Little People, Ghosts."

144 *when something is hot to a human*: Brewster, *The Hill Tribes of Fiji.*

145 *a young son of a king wants a perfect bride*: Dracott, "The Anar Pari, or The Pomegranate Fairy."

145 *this context is important to acknowledge*: See our note on the story itself for more information about why we chose to include Dracott's version.

146 *"essentially an animal spirit"*: Yeats, *Fairy and Folk Tales of the Irish Peasantry.*

146 *"out of a certain hill in Leinster"*: Yeats, *Fairy and Folk Tales of the Irish Peasantry.*

147 *"there is a Welsh tradition"*: Sikes, *British Goblins.*

148 *an atliarusek marries a human girl in secret*: Rink, *Tales and Traditions of the Eskimo.*

148 *actually hunt tiny polar bears*: Claybourne, *The Fairy Atlas.*

150 *"have never been seen since"*: Claybourne, *The Fairy Atlas.*

151 *According to W. R. S. Ralston's 1872 book*: Ralston, *The Songs of the Russian People.*

151 *He never has any eyebrows*: Britannica, "Leshy."

151 *in his true shape, he has horns*: Ralston, *The Songs of the Russian People.*

151 *You can summon a leshy*: Ralston, *The Songs of the Russian People.*

151 *leshy of the cornfields*: Ralston, *The Songs of the Russian People.*

152 *Some identified by Katharine Briggs*: Briggs, *A Dictionary of Fairies.*

153 *"the death-candle appears"*: Evans-Wentz, *The Fairy-Faith in Celtic Countries.*

153 *"The Will o' the Wisp is an interesting thing"*: Daimler, *A New Dictionary of Fairies.*

154 *"magical in themselves, with special powers"*: Briggs, *The Fairies in Tradition and Literature.*

154 *"are often described as red and white"*: Briggs, *The Fairies in Tradition and Literature.*

155 *"is described in one text as emerald"*: Britannica, "Garuda."

155 *"death to touch"* him: Briggs, *A Dictionary of Fairies.*

156 *in the realm of sculpture*: Britannica, "Yaksha."

157 *they really hate to be disturbed*: Claybourne, *The Fairy Atlas.*

157 *Modern medicine usually doesn't*: Martinez, "The Curse of the Nuno Sa Punso."

159 *"semi-divine being[s] with a human face"*: Ramayana (Sattar translation).

159 *This kingdom is resplendent*: Britannica, "Naga."

159 *"when they became too populous"*: Britannica, "Naga."

161 *"the souls of the trees"*: Claybourne, *The Fairy Atlas.*

161 *"deformed, hairy, and indeed—fairy-like"*: Landry, personal communication.

161 *"how to use plants as medicines"*: Claybourne, *The Fairy Atlas.*

161 *"the shy Aziza retreated deeper"*: Claybourne, *The Fairy Atlas.*

161 *"the source of all divine creativity"*: Politz, *Transforming Vòdún.*

161 *"the force of inspiration"*: Landry, personal communication.

161 *If you're lucky enough*: Our thanks to both Timothy R. Landry and Misty L. Bastian for their insights on the Aziza.

163 *"The Anar Pari, or Pomegranate Fairy"*: Dracott, "The Anar Pari."

## CHAPTER 5: FAIRY NEIGHBORS

171 *"the ancestral fairy who is attached"*: Briggs, *The Fairies in Tradition and Literature*.

172 *"the term shedim may derive from"*: Ben-Amos, "On Demons."

172 *shedim "possess the feet and claws"*: Carlson, "Notes on a Demonic Pantheon."

173 *the menehune did not appear in stories recorded*: Martins, "Menehune."

174 *"the gentlest of all"*: Briggs, *The Fairies in Tradition and Literature*.

174 *"The selkie story calls out to us for justice"*: Miller, "Sea Lion Woman."

176 *"near mirror-images of those humans"*: Gunnell, "Introduction."

176 *"Some people put small shelters"*: Claybourne, *The Fairy Atlas*.

177 *The jogah are small fairies*: We're referring to them as "jogah" here, but as John Witthoft and Wendell S. Hadlock point out, the six nations actually each refer to the same creature by different names. "Jogah" or "jogáo" is the Seneca word specifically, which we are using here because it seems to be the most well known.

177 *they're likely to go about in pairs*: Witthoft and Hadlock, "Cherokee-Iroquois Little People."

177 *some jogah who help a small girl*: Claybourne, *The Fairy Atlas*.

178 *"a diminutive supernatural being of Irish folklore"*: Ó Giolláin, "The Leipreachán and Fairies."

178 *He considers leprechauns to be "the artisans"*: Ó Giolláin, "The Leipreachán and Fairies," quoting Philip Dixon Hardy.

178 *"he seems to observers to be old"*: Ó Giolláin, "The Leipreachán and Fairies."

178 *"Red is by far the [leprechaun's] favorite color"*: Ó Giolláin, "The Leipreachán and Fairies."

178 *They love tobacco*: Ó Giolláin, "The Leipreachán and Fairies."

179 *"a pot of silver, a pot of money"*: Ó Giolláin, "The Leipreachán and Fairies."

180 *The legend is known throughout China*: You can also find a very similar and popular version of this story called "The Cowherd and the Weaver Girl," but the "weaver girl" in that tale does not always seem to be a fairy or even fairylike being.

180 *But once a year*: Claybourne, *The Fairy Atlas*.

180 *this legend has a fairly complicated history*: Idema, *The Metamorphosis of Tianxian Pei*.

180 *the story "is so well-known in China"*: Holm, "The Exemplar of Filial Piety."

181 *The konderong comes from the Wolof culture*: Misty L. Bastian tells us that across West Africa, and even further, spirits can be identified because there's something unusual about their feet. They may be backward-facing, cloven-hoofed, or otherwise unexpected.

181 *they're fond of pranks*: Claybourne, *The Fairy Atlas*.

181 *If you can steal their calabash*: Claybourne, *The Fairy Atlas*.

183 *In Barbara Rieti's monograph*: Rieti, *Strange Terrain*.

183 *Peter Narváez even goes so far*: Narváez, "Newfoundland Berry Pickers."

183 *If you cross them*: Claybourne, *The Fairy Atlas*.

184 *He usually wears mining gear*: Claybourne, *The Fairy Atlas*.

184 *"muki" comes from the Quechuan*: Faries, "The Mischievous Muki." We are delighted to tell you that Faries's article was originally published in *CIM Magazine*, the magazine for the Canadian Institute of Mining, Metallurgy and Petroleum. Kudos to the CIM for embracing mining folklore!

184 *the muki is a truly amoral fairy*: Claybourne, *The Fairy Atlas*.

185 *"he punishes those who do not observe"*: Kononenko, *Slavic Folklore*.

185 *Should they be foolish enough*: Kononenko, *Slavic Folklore*.

186 *the first mention of these fairies in English*: Werner, "Abatwa Tradition."

186 *Though they were small enough*: Callaway, *Nursery Tales, Traditions*.

186 *they hate to be told that they're small*: Claybourne, *The Fairy Atlas*.

186 *"uncanny reputation as sorcerers"*: Werner, "Abatwa Tradition."

188 *they usually live in a society*: Keightley, *The Fairy Mythology*.

188 *"wear clothes of moss"*: Claybourne, *The Fairy Atlas*.

188 *The "next morning"*: Keightley, *The Fairy Mythology*.

189 *their fragile build makes them susceptible*: Claybourne, *The Fairy Atlas*.

189 *"a complex network of knowledge"*: "Indigenous Australians," Australian Museum.

189 *When the first people*: "Indigenous Australians," Australian Museum.

190 *Briggs doesn't limit mermaids to the ocean*: Briggs, *The Fairies in Tradition and Literature*.

191 *"our anxieties about water beings"*: Bacchilega and Brown, *The Penguin Book of Mermaids*.

192 *"probably from a recollection"*: Keightley, *The Fairy Mythology*.

192 *"they marry, have children"*: Keightley, *The Fairy Mythology*.

194 *four kinds of yunwi tsunsdi*: Witthoft and Hadlock, "Cherokee-Iroquois Little People."

194 *"If you find something valuable"*: Claybourne, *The Fairy Atlas*.

195 *"an old-fashioned human"*: Claybourne, *The Fairy Atlas*.

195 *stories of orang bunian women*: Hadler, *Muslims and Matriarchs*.

196 *"often associated with Buddhism"*: Foster, *The Book of Yōkai*. You'll see this in our story for this chapter.

196 *two distinct varieties of tengu*: Foster, *The Book of Yōkai*.

196 *"It is impossible to unpack"*: Foster, *The Book of Yōkai*.

197 *"considered after-death incarnations"*: Foster, *The Book of Yōkai*.

197 *Around the twelfth century*: Foster, *The Book of Yōkai*.

197 *"We can also imagine how Tengu"*: Foster, *The Book of Yōkai*.

198 *"Story of a Tengu"*: Hearn, "Story of a Tengu."

205 *"make it clear that they are not generally conceived"*: Briggs, *The Fairies in Tradition and Literature*.

206 *the changeling tradition is widespread*: Munro, "The Invisible Made Visible."

206 *When they do speak*: Munro, "The Invisible Made Visible."

207 *Susan Schoon Eberly adds*: Eberly, "Fairies and the Folklore of Disability."

207 *"Dazzy Walter, the wife of Abel Walter"*: Sikes, *British Goblins*.

208 *Sikes adds, hilariously*: Sikes, *British Goblins*.

208 *changeling narratives developed as a way to explain*: Munro, "The Invisible Made Visible"; Eberly, "Fairies and the Folklore of Disability."

208 *"the infant or very young child who is different"*: Eberly, "Fairies and the Folklore of Disability."

209 *notably dark skin*: Sikes, *British Goblins*.

209 *"Under the pretense of proving"*: Sikes, *British Goblins*.

210 *"Against it any folklorist puts up"*: Briggs, *The Fairies in Tradition and Literature*.

210 *The fifth and last photograph*: Sugg, "Fairy Magic and the Cottingley Photographs."

210 *England was just coming out of World War I*: Sugg, "Fairy Magic and the Cottingley Photographs."

210 *In 1983, Elsie would even admit*: Sugg, "Fairy Magic and the Cottingley Photographs."

211 *"lived in an underground country"*: Briggs, *The Fairies in Tradition and Literature*.

211 *few mentions of them appeared*: Briggs, *The Fairies in Tradition and Literature*.

212 *"Jimmy Thomas, of Wendron parish"*: Evans-Wentz, *The Fairy-Faith in Celtic Countries*.

212 *"fairies were less intimidating"*: Purkiss, *At the Bottom of the Garden*.

213 *"There nine sisters rule"*: Geoffrey of Monmouth, "La Vita Merlini."

213 *"the French prose romances"*: Spivack, "Morgan Le Fay."

214 *"the human midwife is almost as important"*: Briggs, *The Fairies in Tradition and Literature*.

214 *These were carried away*: Briggs, *The Fairies in Tradition and Literature*.

214 *"[A] farmer went to Llangefni"*: Evans-Wentz, *The Fairy-Faith in Celtic Countries*.

215 *a midwife being an actual fairy herself*: Evans-Wentz, *The Fairy-Faith in Celtic Countries*.

216 *"an early student in folk-lore"*: Lang, "The History of the Book and Author."

216 *"a kind of metaphysic"*: Lang, "The History of the Book and Author."

216 *"Kirk affirms the Second Sight"*: Stewart, *Robert Kirk*.

217 *"at the time of his disappearance"*: Evans-Wentz, *The Fairy-Faith in Celtic Countries*.

217 *"Mrs. J. MacGregor"*: Evans-Wentz, *The Fairy-Faith in Celtic Countries*.

218 *"Tam Lin"*: Child "39A: Tam Lin." This edition is a shorter version of the original *English and Scottish Popular Ballads* edited by Francis James Child and originally published in five volumes from 1882 to 1898. According to the book's preface, it "offers a selection from the materials collected and edited by Mr. Child, and is prepared in accordance with a plan which he had approved."

218 *"To come or gae by Carterhaugh"*: Sound familiar? Yes, this is where we got the name of our school!

## CONCLUSION: THE RUMORS HAVE BEEN GREATLY EXAGGERATED

223 *"fairies were and continue to be"*: Bourke, "The Virtual Reality of the Irish Fairy Legend."

223 *Shakespeare played a "pivotal role"*: Purkiss, *At the Bottom of the Garden.*

224 *"a procession of creatures"*: Briggs, *The Fairies in Tradition and Literature.*

224 *"his refusal to know"*: Purkiss, *At the Bottom of the Garden.*

224 *"restores fully a sense of the otherness"*: Briggs, *The Fairies in Tradition and Literature.*

224 *We do, however, get*: Purkiss, *At the Bottom of the Garden.*

224 *Other notable contributions*: Diane Purkiss writes, "When we think of Victorian fairies, what comes first to mind is probably a poem, or a painting, or a children's book. But for many Victorians, particularly early Victorians, fairies would have conjured up a vision of theatrical splendor" (Purkiss, *At the Bottom of the Garden*). For more on this, we recommend Jennifer Schacker's book *Staging Fairyland.*

224 *Even in the realist work of the period*: Warman, *The Fae, the Fairy Tale, and the Gothic Aesthetic.*

225 *"the people who knew what tradition was"*: Briggs, *The Fairies in Tradition and Literature.*

225 *"Besides, what you call them"*: Kipling, *Puck of Pook's Hill.*

225 *Katharine Briggs considered Tolkien's books*: Briggs, *The Fairies in Tradition and Literature.*

226 *"This feisty little pixie"*: Alexander, *Fairies.*

226 *a star on the Hollywood Walk of Fame*: Alexander, *Fairies.*

227 *"quite authentic"*: Purkiss, *At the Bottom of the Garden.*

228 *Fairylore and belief can also be found*: Butler, "The Sídhe and Fairy Forts."

229 *"a secular version of the same"*: Young, "A History of the Fairy Investigation Society."

# ACKNOWLEDGMENTS

This book would not have been possible without the work of the folklorists, anthropologists, historians, and collectors who precede us. We thank every single scholar and writer who appears in our (fully out-of-control) bibliography. In particular, we're indebted to:

Katharine Briggs and Diane Purkiss, the queens of writing beautifully, scholastically, and holistically about fairylore.

W. Y. Evans-Wentz, Thomas Crofton Croker, W. B. Yeats, and Thomas Keightley for their magical, foundational collections and writings.

Anna Claybourne, who wrote an incredibly charming and soundly researched book on global fairylore for children! Her book pointed us toward many creatures we might have otherwise overlooked.

Michael Dylan Foster, for making Japanese folklore so accessible with his captivating accounts of the Yōkai.

Natalie Kononenko, for so expertly presenting Slavic folklore.

Morgan Daimler, for wading through truly endless misinformation to accurately represent Celtic fairies and her unerring fakelore detection, as well as her wonderful research.

We cannot recommend all of their work highly enough. If you need more books after reaching the end of *Fairylore*, you know where to go next!

A special shoutout to Misty L. Bastian, a sociocultural anthropologist who specializes in the study of African religions and gender, and Timothy R. Landry, a professor of anthropology and religious studies, who so graciously consulted with us on our African fairies to make sure we represented them as accurately as possible. And another to Meenoo Mishra, our fabulous and knowledgeable virtual assistant, who helped us in the same way with our Indian fairies.

Thank you to our editor, Kate Zimmermann, who dreamed of a book like this, and our agent, Adriana Stimola, who has been an endlessly enthusiastic and supportive advocate throughout this entire process (#teenwitchesforlife). Thank you to Annie Stegg and Kristin Kwan for their absolutely stunning art. And thank you to the entire team at Sterling Ethos and Hachette for getting this book over the finish line.

Finally, thank you to our families, friends, colleagues, former professors, and cats. We couldn't do any of this without you all. Special shout-outs to our respective partners: Jared Jones, who keeps Sara sane with his brilliance, humor, and mad proofing skills, and Joshua Mears, whose insight into the world of Faerie constantly inspires and delights Brittany; to our parents, who wholeheartedly supported this whole "I'm going to be a folklorist!" thing with actual enthusiasm; to Margaret Yocom, who cultivated our love for folklore and inspired us to always think outside the box; to Mary McMyne, who saved our bacon; to Gypsy Thornton, Deborah Sage, C. S. E. Cooney, and the Sisterhood of the Moon for always getting us; to Erin and Michael Bahl for the feasts and friendship; to Sara Dann for helping us stay afloat during the chaos; to all the amazing students of Carterhaugh; and to Terri Windling, the queen of fairies herself.

Any errors in this book are our own.

# INDEX

AMY PARRISH

# ABOUT THE AUTHORS

DR. SARA CLETO and DR. BRITTANY WARMAN are award-winning folklorists, teachers, and writers with a combined twenty-six years in higher education and over a hundred publications. After earning their PhDs in English and Folklore from the Ohio State University, they founded the Carterhaugh School of Folklore and the Fantastic, teaching creative souls how to reenchant their lives through folklore and fairy tales. In 2019, Carterhaugh won the Dorothy Howard Award for Folklore and Education from the American Folklore Society. When they aren't teaching at Carterhaugh, they are scholars, writers, and best friends who have published peer-reviewed articles; appeared on podcasts; sold stories and poems; written academic articles, book introductions, and encyclopedia entries; and written for magazines and blogs. (They've also been known to crush "Total Eclipse of the Heart" at karaoke.) They are regular writers for *Enchanted Living Magazine*, created a series on *Dracula* for the Great Courses, and have delivered lectures at venues like the Smithsonian Associates, the Library of Congress, the Profs & Pints series, the Maryland Renaissance Festival, the Dublin Irish Festival, the Contemporary American Theater Festival, and FaerieCon. They love cats, chai, red lipstick, and bringing magic into the everyday. You can visit them online at www.carterhaughschool.com.